ALLA RENÉE BOZARTH

Wisdom and Wonderment

CompCare® Publishers

Library of Congress Cataloging-in-Publication Data
Bozarth, Alla Renée
    Wisdom and wonderment: thirty-one feasts to nourish your soul/Alla
Renée Bozarth.
      p. cm.
      ISBN 0-89638-360-1
1. Spiritual life. 2. Devotional calendars. I. Title.
BL624.B6293   1993
291.4'3—dc20   93-4153
                                                CIP

Cover design by Garborg Design Work
Interior design by Leah Peterson
Edited by Linda Christensen, Ph.D.

Inquiries, orders, and catalog requests should be addressed to
CompCare Publishers
3850 Annapolis Lane, Suite 100
Minneapolis, MN 55447
Call 612/559-4800
or toll free 800/328-3330

I wish to thank and bless my publishers and editors for their kindness and sensitivity—especially the council of seven who heartstormed for the inspiration to name this book.

My special thanks to Leah Peterson for her artistic eye, to Jane Noland for her long-time faithfulness to excellence, and to Dr. Linda Christensen for her loving labor in serving the feasts.

The Banquet Table

1. A Feast of Honor
2. A Feast of Respect
3. A Feast of Communing
4. A Feast of Humility
5. A Feast of Gratitude
6. A Feast of Choice
7. A Feast of Acceptance
8. A Feast of Simplicity
9. A Feast of Listening
10. A Feast of Sharing
11. A Feast of Learning
12. A Feast of Foolishness
13. A Feast of Attention
14. A Feast of Healing
15. A Feast of Giving
16. A Feast of Action
17. A Feast of Forgiveness
18. A Feast of Surprise
19. A Feast of Compassion
20. A Feast of Relaxation
21. A Feast of Happiness
22. A Feast of Wonder
23. A Feast of Possibilities
24. A Feast of Mercy
25. A Feast of the Wild
26. A Feast of Grace
27. A Feast of Trust
28. A Feast of Tenderness
29. A Feast of Balance
30. A Feast of Harmony
31. A Feast of Celebration

Desserts for after the Feast

Acknowledgments

"Be," and "What Jesus Really Said," were first on the audiotape, "Reading out Loud to God," Wisdom House, 43222 S.E. Tapp Road, Sandy, Oregon 97055, 1990.

All quotations noted as *Hebrew Scripture, New Testament, Prayer of Manasseh, and Book of Wisdom* are from *The Holy Bible, New Revised Standard Version*, Oxford University Press, New York, 1989.

Quotations noted as *Tao Te Ching* were taken from *Tao Te Ching*, translated from the Chinese by Stephen Mitchell, Harper and Row, New York, 1988.

The term *addiction to perfection* is used in Feast 7 with gratitude to Marion Woodman who wrote the brilliant book, *Addiction to Perfection*, Inner City Books, Toronto, 1982.

The quote on Feast 17 comes from *The Hymnal 1982*, The Church Hymnal Corporation, New York, 1982.

"Love Mantra for Letting Go" was taken from *Life Is Goodbye/Life Is Hello, Revised Edition*, CompCare Publishers, Minneapolis, 1986.

Quotations noted as *WomanWitness* were taken from *WomanWitness: A Feminist Lectionary and Psalter by Miriam Therese Winter*, illustrated by Meinrad Craighead, The Crossroad Publishing Company, New York, 1992.

Introduction

"Life's a banquet and most poor suckers are starving."
Rosalind Russell as Auntie Mame

This book is an invitation to awareness and to life. It is offered in the hope that the reflections it contains will help you feel welcome at the feast of life. May they serve to remind you that Grace comes in many flavors. And may you leave this book hungry, lonely, and empty no longer.

We often have the experience of starving when truly we are surrounded by pastures of plenty. Our hungry hearts long to be filled and our starving souls yearn for nourishing sustenance so, while we live in a world of abundance, we feel lonely, purposeless, and empty. How, then, can we open ourselves to see and to make room for the things we truly need to come into our lives to heal and fulfill us? How can we approach the abundant banquet and allow ourselves to be nourished and fed?

Sit and rest yourself for a while, and open your heart in quiet regard. Allow yourself to breathe and, as you inhale, breathe in complete awareness. Do you feel your body being filled with air, which gives you life? Stay in this moment; continue to be aware. Let yourself believe you are a valuable living part of the universe that contains you.

With each breath you receive, you are given the gift of life. You give back the gift of life with each breath you release. One complete breath is one complete act of receiving and giving. You have engaged in this miracle from the moment of your birth.

We breathe, but most often we are not aware—nor do we appreciate—that we breathe.

We have not learned to give ourselves to the awareness, nor do we allow our souls to fill with wonder at the miracle in which we live with each breath of our lives.

It is simple to begin. It takes a single decision. We simply must decide to do what we normally do, but do it with awareness. Once there is awareness, the same breath, the same air seems transformed, even radiant, because now we recognize it; now we are present for it. Now we know it is a miracle.

Diverse spiritual practices offer paths of discipline leading to unfolding awareness. The great spiritual traditions throughout human history and prehistory have common themes which hold constant:

- Reverence for life
- Remembrance of the Great Mystery
- Belief in a Creator of all that is
- Loving respect and compassion for others
- Gratitude for every moment of life

Jews have guidelines for living these themes in the Torah, the essence of which is to love and serve the One God, and to love one's neighbor as oneself. Christian tradition shares the same essential guideline, continuing a tradition of creation-centered gratitude and a sense of wonderment at the unfolding miracle of birth, death, and resurrection.

Muslims consecrate their lives to a Creator who is merciful and compassionate. Hindus celebrate life in a rich appreciation of the many forms of the divinity which shape and fill the created universe. Buddhists focus on the expression of reverence and strive to live in mindfulness: Be mindful to refrain from causing harm; be mindful to help bring about good.

Threads of compassion and wisdom braid themselves through other Eastern traditions, as they do also in the nature-centered religious traditions of Africa and the Americas.

Ancient Taoism appreciates the continuous interplay and oneness of opposites: always day eats the night, always night eats the day. All that is young becomes old, and all that is old grows young again in new forms.

At the heart of all of these spiritual traditions is the call to wakefulness and to awareness. The call is there to be present to the miracle of our lives, centered with every breath, centered in every moment. Paradoxically, we are most awake and aware when we are relaxed and rested. We even find awareness eases suffering. Soon we can be open to awareness at all levels of being: thinking, feeling, sensing, intuiting, judging, perceiving, acting.

So, again, sit, rest, and breathe. Let yourself rest in awareness. Breathe out all tensions and cares. Trust the moment to hold you. Trust life to sustain and to carry you. Allow yourself to be held. Breathe deeply, completely. Envision your heart's greatest desire and offer it to the Creative Spirit to be blessed. Be relaxed and open, relaxed enough to be taken by surprise, open enough to be delighted by the feasts of love and grace which are presented to you. Go slowly, so that you do not miss them when they come. Breathe gently. Do not strain to look too hard. Let soft eyes regard the gifts and a calm heart respond.

Feast upon confidence.

Feast upon wonder.

Feast upon mystery.

Feast upon renewal.

Feast upon the unexpected.

Feast upon the gifts all around you and within you, all the strong, sweet, bitter, and salty flavors of life.

Through the rich flavors of life's experiences, it is possible to choose to grow in wisdom and to be inspired. It is possible to be transformed more and more into your truest, deepest self, and to experience the Loving Creator's dream for you come true. Even tragic losses can fertilize future goodness. Life is not given to us to be a burden, to cause endless effort, or to be endured. Sometimes it contains all these elements, but primarily it is a precious gift to be enjoyed.

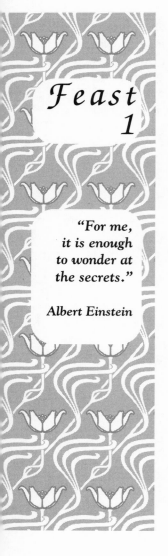

"*For me,
it is enough
to wonder at
the secrets.*"

Albert Einstein

*L*et yourself remember who you really are.

- You are a child of God.
- You are of infinite value.
- You are a dream come true.

No matter what human drama you were born into, no matter what conflict was acted out in your personal family history, Life accepted and welcomed you at the moment of your birth. The fact that Life continued to sustain you, sometimes against all odds, is a sign that God wants you here, just as the whole of the universe continues to want you.

Life is prepared to receive and welcome you anew each day. As a treasured member of the human family, Life's welcome comes to you through the sunlight that shines on your face and in the air that fills your lungs and offers you life.

Welcome also comes to you in every human smile and in every act of kindness extended to you. It comes through the warmth of an animal's fur as you stroke it and in the delighted wagging tail that greets you. Every flower, tree, river, and waterfall welcomes you and invites you to feel wonder.

Life's welcome comes to you through your own inner ability to see wonder, to feel gratitude, and fill your soul with joy. It comes through your power to love in return. Soon, you know you are the flower and fruit of a seed planted by a Divine Gardener: God's dream come true.

You are a spiritual presence on the Earth. Your destiny is . . .

- ❧ to grow in harmony with all life.
- ❧ to fulfill your human potential.
- ❧ to love and to be loved.
- ❧ to discover and to use your gifts.
- ❧ to experience yourself as a vital contribution to the well-being of all.

Then, having remembered who you really are, celebrate and cherish your life. Cherish the mystery of being a complex living organism delicately balanced in a miraculous body. Celebrate being a thinking intellect and a feeling soul, both alive and growing within your mortal body.

Celebrate and honor God in you, and honor and celebrate your Self in God. You have both large Self and small self contained within what you think of as truly *you*. Your small self is your ego, it is your image or the mask to which you fearfully cling and then show to the world.

But your large Self is all that you are and all that you can become in the Mind and Heart of God. Your large Self is free from vanity and fear; it is accepting and glad to be a part of the infinite pattern of creation. It is content to dwell in the present and eager to learn in the future. To unfold and grow, your large Self needs to be fed with love, kindness, and respect. It needs this nourishment from others and from you.

Health and well-being thrive on love. Love can be channeled through others when their love meets the love already in you. It joins, fills, and enriches your life. When you have love from within yourself and from others, your heart responds with feelings of joy and peace. Filled with love, peace, and joy, it is easy to remember who you really are: a child of God who is of infinite value and who is daily welcomed anew by an abundant universe.

 Thou shalt not insult thy Creator by hating, abusing, or disrespecting thy Self.

Feast 2

*I*n Hebrew and Christian tradition, the essence of a life well-lived is summarized in these wise words: Love your neighbor as yourself. As we recognize that we are wanted, loved, and welcomed by the Creator, by the very Life that gives us life, we realize that every living being is equally wanted, loved, and welcomed. We begin to see that each of us truly needs love, kindness and respect.

Often, though, we disregard our neighbors in the midst of crowded hours, busy days, and busy lives. We are inattentive and closed to them. We defend ourselves against others by viewing each person as a possible intrusion or annoyance. We close our senses and our hearts to other presences. Sometimes, when we do actually see and hear others, we perceive them as negative images of ourselves. Because we are unable to love ourselves, we see others as being unlovable in the same way.

The basis for all prejudice and hatred of others is actually hatred of ouselves. Too painful to be experienced directly, we project our self-hatred outwardly onto others, who then carry the unclaimed and shameful parts of ourselves. Usually it is easier to project our self-hatred onto those who seem sufficiently different from us in some way. Then we can reassure ourselves: they are different; they are bad. Therefore we are good.

Only when the projection is recognized and called home can self-healing begin. As we come to know, forgive, and accept ourselves, we can stop hating others. As we commit ourselves to our own healing and growth, we also become able to know and to accept others and to ask for and receive forgiveness from those we may have injured or treated unjustly through our own ignorance and fear.

One of the most freeing experiences of life is to have a prejudice exposed and healed. This usually happens by surprise, when we least expect it. We may not even be aware that we have harbored a negative and rejecting attitude toward others. But when beauty breaks forth from a new source in ways that cannot be denied, our distorted mirror is shattered. We become free to see the true image of ourselves and of others. Fear and rigidity give way to an acceptance of our true Self. The other whom we rejected in fear becomes someone who, with us, is God's dream come true, a mystery to cherish, a living being struggling; one who is in need of infinite tenderness. Fear and rigidity are transformed from distorted mirrors into clear windows through which we truly see one another. Sometimes the windows open, and we are able to invite each other into new and wonder-filled worlds. Then our lives become marvelously enriched; our freedom to move and grow becomes enhanced.

In India, people greet one another with a sacred word: Namaste. This means that God within me honors God within you. In saying this to another person, it becomes impossible to treat the other with anything less than loving kindness and respect. It is a declaration of utmost well-wishing and reverence for the mystery of the other, a cherishing of the life that radiates from within the other.

Look, first, into yourself. Look into a mirror in your home and see through the visible features of your face into your vulnerable, but unspeakably exquisite inner soul. Soften your facial muscles into a kind smile, look through your own reflected eyes, and say, "Namaste!"

Then turn to the other precious people in your world, and again say, "Namaste: God within me honors God within you." And, then to strangers . . . "Namaste." With all your heart, say to every other, "I wish you well." Feel the creative power of love move through you; notice that as it moves, it blesses you.

 Thou shalt not insult thy Creator by hating, abusing, or disrespecting
any Other Child of God.

Feast 3

Words are magical. Words tell stories, create worlds, unite lovers, delight friends, dismay enemies, teach skills, define culture, describe mystery, shape dreams, inspire, infuriate, bring tears and laughter, and change lives.

In loving someone and growing close in a family, in friendship, or in committed erotic love, the need arises to hear and say certain nurturing words, without which hearts and spirits starve. We hunger for the right words! We long to have them spoken by those we love.

Words are acts, acts that need to be accompanied by movements of the body and attitudes of mind. If there is disparity among any of these three elements—voice, body movements, or attitudes—the words are seen as lies. "I love you," needs to be accompanied by warm eyes and a soft touch. Also, loving acts and attitudes often need to be accompanied by the words, "I love you." When words don't match actions, or when actions are not verbalized, confusion and mistrust result. Our inner life thrives on a diet rich in praise and on words of love. To survive, we need attention, affection, and appreciation and to hear those things expressed in words.

Giving and receiving praise and words of love bring comfort, affirmation, and nurturing feelings to both the giver and the receiver. Relationships are also strengthened through the free expression of love. Words need to originate in the heart and to be given flesh as they are spoken. They need to live and to be true.

Loved ones speak to each other in ways that are comfortable and routine. Feelings of tenderness and affection become sustaining words spoken on the way to the daycare center, over dinner, or during twilight walks on soft spring nights. Our hearts and souls long for connection with the hearts and souls of those whom we love. Hearts and souls long for connection, as well, with the Source of Love.

Every day, "I love you," must be said, savored, and experienced. Solitary periods of life may not offer you daily intimate contact with others. But intimacy with creation and with the Source of creation can be fed and fostered each day.

The longing for connection, the deepest longing of the heart, is prayer: it is intimacy with the Creator. Those brought up in formal religious traditions may associate prayer with the formularized worship experience of gathering together with others and speaking the same words to God with one voice. Those words were important because traditional words linked us with the spiritual ancestors who themselves used these same words as they addressed the Holy Other. Prayer words created a spiritual bond with human beings in the present and with others in times past who sought to connect with the essence of the Divine. Over time, through words of prayer, forms of communication with God and with others evolved. When the words were true and penetrating, they opened the sacred silence of a shared Presence.

Just as beloved children are always held in the heart and mind of their mother and yet are separate from her, Divinity is experienced as separate and beyond us, but also as a reality within us. As intimately as blood in veins and marrow in bones, others and the Holy Other are part of us when we love.

And, because God is experienced as both within and beyond, we can relate to God in both ways.

To use the words of the tradition to which you belong is to affirm formally that you are speaking in the context of that tradition. But remember that it is also possible to speak just for yourself! And because you sense God both within and beyond, you can

communicate what is in your heart in your own true way: through attitude, attention, actions of your body, and through your own words of love. Cry or laugh your prayer; sing your prayer; dance, run, sweat your prayer; or just be still, enjoying the presence of the One who loves. You have a right to speak with God in your own language.

Allow yourself to find your own voice and your own words to share your deeper, larger Self with the Creator. Put your body into it. Let your bones speak. Let your muscles pray. Make a noise! Move! Write God a love letter. Read out loud. Sing God a love song. Rage in anger. Give forth! Hold nothing back. Or be sweetly still in the Presence.

Your relationship to the Divine is the most intimate relationship possible.

 Thou shalt not bore thy Creator by reading from a script to converse with Same—unless it be to share good literature, for the Creator loves a good read.

Feast 4

There is a story of a devout young rabbi who, one day after sabbath services, found himself alone in his synagogue. The building was simple in design, yet constructed with such love and reverence that every piece of wood, every stone in its structure was beautiful and inspired devotion. As sunlight filled the sanctuary, revealing every subtle hue in the marble column near the rabbi's feet, he fell to his knees and began to speak loudly to God. "O God, Ruler of the Universe," he began, "though I am the lowest of your servants and not worthy of Your consideration, yet consider me. Though I am a speck of dust and of no value, indeed, the very most despicable of all beings, hear my prayer."

Although the young rabbi didn't know it, the caretaker happened to be silently mopping on the other side of the pillar. When he heard the rabbi's words, he peered around the pillar and saw the young rabbi on his knees. At that same moment, the senior rabbi also happened to come in, and he, too, heard and saw the young rabbi in his humble prayer. The elder rabbi, inspired by his colleague's fervor, fell to his knees and began to beat his breast and cry out, "O God, Ruler of the Universe, I beg you to look upon me, your most worthless servant, with mercy!"

Now the caretaker could contain his own emotion no longer. Moved to expression, he also fell to his knees, saying, "O God, O God, look at me, your most lowly, your most worthless creature. Take pity on my unworthiness." The young rabbi turned, watched the caretaker a moment, and then with a shrug said to the senior rabbi, "Look who thinks he's unworthy!"

18

There can be a kind of perverse glory in believing ourselves to be the worst of something, especially if we are quite certain that we are not the best. It is, perhaps, still a matter of being the best but being the best at being bad. Even if we win the proverbial booby prize, at least we've won something. Perhaps our boasts of incompetence and unworthiness are really bids for attention and sympathy, as we hope that someone will argue, "No! No! You're the best!" Or at least, "You're not so bad, really."

There are those times when each of us does experience serious self-doubts or even unworthiness. But even then, we do not really want anyone else to agree with us. We still wish to be reassured.

At the same time, if we have betrayed our own values or caused injury to another, guilt and sorrow may be justified. What we need then is to find a way to make amends as best as we can and to seek forgiveness. But this kind of sincere remorse is far removed from the self-centered denial of worth that many of us may still believe our God enjoys hearing (or human observers find impressive).

Our notion of the nature or personality of the Creator matures as we mature, for we inevitably create God in our own image. We are limited human beings who, when confronted with our limitations, may compensate by viewing our Higher Power as having the same limitations. As immature humans, we may create an immature god-image.

It is difficult to imagine a god who would actually enjoy seeing anyone grovel. This simply does not fit with the qualities of mercy and unconditional love we consensually attribute to our Creator. It is really much easier to imagine a God with divine impatience, saying, "Stop that! Get up on your feet and be you. I can't stand that groveling!"

What does it say about the One in whose image we think we are created if we think we are worthless? In the eyes of God, and through the lens of eternity, there is no hierarchy

of souls: each of us is of infinite value. And each of us is but a single bit of stardust in the vastness of creation.

The philosopher Martin Buber told a tale of a certain zaddik, a wise and just person. The zaddik encountered a pilgrim on the road who asked, "What is the truth of human nature?" The zaddik's answer came, as most answers concerning ultimate truth must come, in a metaphor:

"Every human being needs an invisible vest with two pockets. With this vest, you could reach into one pocket and pull out a piece of paper with a message written on it: 'You are less than a speck of dust.' Immediately, you must reach into the other pocket and read the message waiting there: 'You are the center of the universe.' In the mind of God, it doesn't matter which message you read first, as long as you read them both together, for neither one alone is true, but both together—that is the truth."

In your mind's eye, put on your invisible vest. Remember throughout each day to take a moment to reach into both pockets. As you ponder their messages, you will see it is really one message. Your true nature is paradoxical: a speck of dust and the center of the universe. Try to accept your own mystery, as God accepts you. Try to accept that, when it is the center of the universe, even a speck of dust need not grovel.

 Thou shalt not grovel.

> *"Let us come into God's presence with thanksgiving; Let us make a joyful noise to God with praise."*
>
> *Psalm 95:2 Hebrew Scriptures*

Whining, as every parent knows, has a negative, grating effect. And as every child knows, it works from time to time. Children often learn that if they can't get what they want by simply asking for it (while being irresistibly cute and appealing), they may get it by wearing down any adult within hearing range. Since we never stop being children, we remain susceptible to the temptation to whine all of our lives, especially when tragedy or fear in the present causes us to remember and relive the fears and tragedies that may have happened in childhood.

Some of us can fall unconsciously into a litany of sorrows and complaints. Our stressed inner child wants a sympathetic adult who will kiss it and make it better. The superficial relief we find when we voice our list of woes is not really satisfying. In burdening someone else with our troubles, we may think we are relieved of them, but that illusion quickly fades. Shallow sympathy is not a substitute for genuine change, and whining just prolongs the pain; it distracts us from our responsibility to take action on our own behalf.

The tyrannical inner child can be greedy for immediate satisfaction and have no sense of limits and boundaries. This child sees the whole world as its anxious attendant, whose only purpose is to serve and please. Any one of us can revert to behaving like a child when we are tired, lonely, or threatened, forgetting all the skills and resources of our adult selves. In pain, we become frantic, clutching greedily to anything or anyone that might bring relief.

Greed is the opposite of gratitude, but gratitude can heal greed. In fact, the emotion of gratitude, with genuine joy at its center, is the most healing of all emotions. I remember my birthday several years ago; I wanted the day to be perfect—no clouds, no crises—just flowing, uninterrupted pleasure. I had been working hard at having my perfect day, and I was singing as I drove to meet a friend for tea. Then I noticed something out of the corner of my eye that did not belong on the road. My brain registered that the jerking shape between the traffic lanes was an animal—a large, beautiful, brown dog that had been hit by a careless human and left to die in agony. I burst into tears, ashamed and enraged with humankind. "God," I prayed, "take it quickly. Don't let it suffer."

Then I realized I could do something else to help. I stopped and called the police, who referred me to Animal Control. I didn't want Animal Control, I wanted Animal Protection! But I proceeded to say, in the fewest words possible, that an animal had been hit and was in great distress and needed help immediately. When I described the location, the woman on the telephone thanked me and disconnected so she could respond. I realized then that I was still crying. The waitress who had let me use the telephone said we should go by the dog and cover it until help arrived.

Because shock had distorted my perception of time and space, the few steps I thought I'd gone were really several blocks. By the time she and I arrived, running and panting, the dog was gone. Someone else had intervened. We both trembled as we walked slowly back to the restaurant together, the other woman holding my arm in a comforting way.

As we walked and talked, I began to realize that I was suffering, too. The greedy child within me that wanted the perfect birthday suddenly overtook the compassionate adult. I blurted out, "It's so hard to see such suffering! It's my birthday!" Without hesitation, my companion responded, "Sometimes being grown up means doing the right thing on your birthday." Instantly, her words of truth and wisdom restored me to my own wise, adult self. I agreed with her, and in my heart I thanked God for her, and for the lesson.

We each have the power to choose our focus: we can increase our misery by making a list of complaints, a litany of personal sorrows; or we can remember that we are truly only a small part of a vast reality, whose combined and individual sorrows are mingled always with gifts and blessings. When we choose to create a litany of thanksgiving, we find deep joy. And when we share our gratitude and joy, we contribute to the healing of others by reminding them of their reasons for gratitude. This healing of others is another gift to be grateful for. Soon, there is no room, nor need, for fear—no need for greed.

The Four Noble Truths of the Buddhist tradition teach that greed is the primary cause of human suffering. Rather than accepting the present condition as an invitation to open up fully to life, we waste our time and energy wishing and whining for life to be something other than what it is. When we take action together and separately to make life better, we have opened ourselves to the possibility of moving from misery into creativity, gratitude, and joy.

Every moment, you can create a litany of thanksgiving, and celebrate all the graces of life with a simple, grateful heart. Open your heart to what you need, and focus on bringing your wishes and actions into harmony with your own present reality. In being grateful, you will find joy. And you will know that you have begun to use your creative power to change the world for the better.

 Thou shalt not whine.

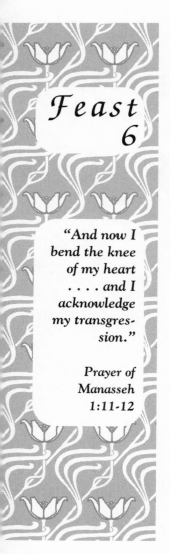

"*And now I bend the knee of my heart . . . . and I acknowledge my transgression.*"

Prayer of Manasseh 1:11-12

Someone once said that sin is doing the same dumb things over and over. That might be too casual a definition, but it is food for thought. The key idea is that if we do not learn from our mistakes, we continue to make the same mistakes, not because of accidental repetition, but rather because we refuse to learn. If we refuse to learn, we will never do things differently, but continue in error.

In *The Road Less Traveled*, M. Scott Peck called sin *militant ignorance*. A Dutch definition expands the idea saying that *sin is the refusal to grow in the direction which conscience dictates*. In all cases, there is the sense of a deliberate, even willful, disregard of our own knowledge of what is good—of what leads to wholeness for ourselves and others—and a disregard of the greater good in which we all live and move and have our being.

Always, sin is separation and severance. Always, it is the rejection of our most true selves.

I am reminded of the story of Lenny on his death bed. As he drifted in and out of consciousness, Lenny made several trips back and forth across the bridge between the realities of time and eternity. One time he met God on the other side. He trembled, terrified that God would be angry at him because he wasn't as wise as Solomon, as brave as Moses, or as compassionate as Jesus. God knew Lenny's fears and said, "Never mind, Lenny. I'm not going to ask you *why* you weren't Solomon, or Moses, or Jesus. Only, please, Lenny, tell me, *why* weren't you Lenny?"

Lenny came back to his body with a wonderful new insight. He told his family, "I know what you have to do in life—become yourself."

We can say, then, that sin is the willful refusal to become yourself, to grow into who you really are when fully realized, alive, creative, loving, and expressing the power of love. Sin is stamping your foot and saying firmly: "No. I'm not going to grow. I'm not going to live out my potential. I'm not going to explore the depths of being and risk ease and security by living fully. I refuse to discover all the possibilities and challenges that might unfold for me. I reject them. I reject life. I reject love. I reject myself."

The result of that declaration is living a limited, utterly wretched life based on a commitment to remain in shallow waters. Such a person stays stuck in stagnant pools, instead of riding the waves and diving deep to the places where dolphins play.

All of us occasionally ignore the wisdom of our souls and follow the path of least resistance. But the moment we notice, the moment we waken from our stupor, we can revise our plans, follow a new map, and change our direction.

Even if a route takes us on wild adventures or offers us wonderful views, it may not be the route, the adventures, or the views that are best for our lives. We all need to be attentive to our own truths and routes, and willing to correct a bad turn as soon as awareness comes.

Sometimes the choices we make or routes we take become habits. Some habits are healthy; other habits are toxic. Toxic habits are often substitutes for what we really need: divine guidance, human comfort, or a change in our lives. Such habits can be addictions, habits that irritate the life right out of us and out of those we love. They irritate love to death and, if untreated, can even lead to physical death.

Addictions may start with a simple thought: "This will be interesting, or fun, or exciting. Or it will guide me off my usual route where I feel so small and unsure." But then we find that the new route, this irritating habit, or death-oriented addiction, is really just a different bad route and that it may be too narrow for us to turn ourselves around easily. We

may have to back all the way out. Or we may need Divine intervention and an airlift at the end of the road.

Open your heart to the conscious awareness of any wrong choices you willfully continue to make or any irritating habits that may endanger the health of any part of your being: your relationships, your emotions, your vocation, your physical body, or your life. Consider how you might make other choices, might change direction or routes and continue on the journey to your best self. Know that you really will have all that you need. Ask for help where it is most appropriate—from loving friends, caring professionals, or the Divine. Be receptive to the wisdom and caring they bring.

 Thou shalt not repeat thy sins and irritating habits over and over again in word or deed.

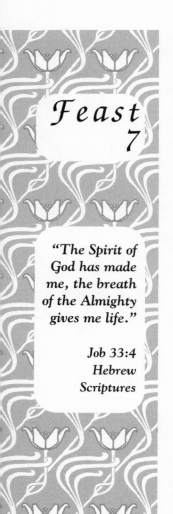

"*The Spirit of God has made me, the breath of the Almighty gives me life.*"

*Job 33:4
Hebrew
Scriptures*

All addictions are deadly. One particularly deadly addiction that most of us don't fully understand is the addiction to perfection. This addiction kills spontaneity, freedom, creativity, and playfulness. It also kills the possibility for joy. Its symptoms are rigidity and futility, judgment and shame, impossible goals and relentless striving, fear and failure. It develops as a way for a frightened child to have the illusion of safety, which, over time, turns the soul to stone.

As children, we all needed affirmation and praise. We needed to know that we were doing and learning enough. We needed to hear that it was enough just to be whoever we were and that mistakes were part of the joy of being human.

Any of us may have grown up never hearing the accepting words, "Well done. Good enough. I'm proud of you. Just your being here brings me delight." So we may spend the rest of our lives frantically trying to win approval and affirmation to make up for the missing messages of childhood. With no positive mirror in our sensitive formative years to show us our beauty, talents, and gifts, we remain anxious within, unsure, never satisfied with ourselves, and compulsively driven to please others. Without the mirror, we remain unable to discern our inherent goodness and the light within.

During times when we feel emotionally unsafe, our addiction to perfection worsens as feelings of powerlessness push us to try to control others, our environment, and ourselves. The morning of my husband's death was the most powerless and chaotic time of my life. Friends had come to sit with me and make tea—which I could not drink—and offer me morsels of food—which I could not eat. When the time came for me to go to the airport and begin the long journey I needed to take, I stopped to dry off every drop of water on the kitchen counter and in the sink. I was self-aware enough to realize that what I was doing seemed insane, and that my loving friends must surely be concerned, so I said to them, "Today, my whole world blew up. In a small way, I need to feel that I can have an effect on something. I know what I'm doing looks crazy, but it does help a little."

I was struggling to feel safe by fighting back with whatever symbolic control I could muster. My regression into my own addiction to perfection during the worst possible stress was like the twitching of a hand after an electrocution. It was a primal, if futile, protest against the capricious violence with which life sometimes shatters our reality. What I really needed was to wail into the profound chaos, not to fight it. Healing began only when I could express my true pain and sacrifice my illusionary addiction to perfection.

There is a superstitious, perverse logic in perfectionism: If I follow all the rules and achieve perfection, I will be perfectly lovable. If I am perfect, I will be perfectly accepted, perfectly taken care of, and perfectly loved.

Operating on that logic, who could abandon the illusion of perfection?

What we fail to grasp is that perfection is not only impossible, it is not even lovable. Not only is perfection not an option for human beings, but even the Creator must consider it boring or every clover would have four leaves.

Native Americans and many other older, wiser cultures around the world have preserved ritual reminders that only the Creator has the right to perfection. Native American art sometimes uses a deliberately flawed or missing bead called the Spirit Bead to show this. The so-called "Persian Flaw" in rug-making has the same meaning. European women in colonial America customarily left a drop of their own blood in a corner of one quilt square, not as a signature, but as an affirmation that life is a dynamic process requiring

sacrifice and mess in the creation of beauty.

When my Steinway grand piano was rebuilt, the technician showed me the hidden places on the underside and inside of the instrument where each person who had originally worked on its construction had left a signature, mark, or initials. Every time an artist signs a crafted work, it is not just an act of ownership or vanity, but also an acknowledgment that no humanly created object is absolutely unadulterated. Life leaves marks, and nothing escapes the mess that is the prerequisite for birth, healing, restoration, or renewal.

Acknowledging this reality, we then understand that the pursuit of perfection is the pursuit of death, for only in death is there no change and no mess. Only in death can nothing more be done.

Overcoming the addiction to perfection requires being open to limitation and incompleteness. It requires not doing things perfectly but well enough. That is not to say that excellence is a futile goal. Excellence comes at that moment when we recognize that something is complete, yet still dynamic. It is actualized and full—but not over-filled or past completion.

Practice imperfection: be real, really you. Make an offering to the universe, and leave some tiny part of it flawed or unfinished. Let it be complete as it is. Accept it. Accept yourself. Know that the universe accepts imperfection as it accepts you. Practice will never make perfect, but practicing imperfection as a spiritual offering will make peace of mind.

 Thou shalt relinquish thine addiction to perfection, for it can only harm thee.

Feast 8

We all want to cling to our comforting delusions. They enable us to survive the terrors of daily life by not allowing more reality than we can bear. As false perceptions lead to false conclusions and as images shape beliefs, illusion feeds delusion. The illusion of stillness on our little planet, which is really moving on its axis around the sun at 40,000 miles per second, keeps us from being dizzy and, indeed, from being deathly afraid. So we share a delusion that all matter is stable, that the world is a still and secure place in which our own spot is fixed and defined.

In spite of the human intellect's marvelous capacity for conceptualization and computation, scientists have not yet formulated the elusive "Grand Unifying Theory," which would resolve all contradictions and explain the true nature of the universe. Perhaps our consciousness needs time to evolve gently into that understanding, or perhaps it is a grand delusion to think that we could ever fully explain the nature of the universe.

Western and Eastern traditions alike have articulated spiritual models that include an intermediate zone following physical death. This is based on the belief that Heaven is so spectacularly different from our world that, if we went straight from here to there, the shock would overwhelm us. Similarly, we all ease ourselves into shocking reality in our daily lives with stories, delusions, distractions, and denial. The ability to do so is truly a creative gift of our merciful minds.

Philosopher Ernest Becker's book, *The Denial of Death*, shows how we, as humans, experience a shattering paradox regarding our own nature. First, we perceive that we are astonishing beings, capable of amazing creative and perceptual powers, and that we are as gods. Paradoxically, we live in mortal bodies subject to death, disease, and grotesque injury—bodies which also engage in daily actions that mortify our grandiose self-image: we are gods who defecate.

In order to live with this terrible contradiction, we have devised a corporate lie: We are as gods, and we don't defecate. There may be some comfort in this lie, but, along with comfort, we also develop neuroses as we hide and feel ashamed of normal functions common to all.

We view ourselves either as inflated beings who could belong to the angelic realm if it weren't for our bodies, or as deflated beings who are ashamed because of the body's natural workings. We may then conclude: we defecate, and God hates us. Through our delusion, we are on a psychic see-saw, bouncing between self-abasement and self-hatred on the one hand and grandiosity and self-inflation on the other.

We also do this as individuals. Because we are so small and the universe is so large, we can sometimes feel afraid and ask, as a child might, "Is life safe, really?" Truly, life is risky, but it is wonderful, too. There are no guarantees against feeling pain, but along with the possibilities of pain are the possibilities of joy, delight, wonder, and bliss. We do not need to be ashamed or afraid. Nor do we need to pretend that we are gods in charge of everything. Let us simply acknowledge our small part, take responsibility for it, and loosen our grip on tightly-held delusions. All the while let us be open to the knowledge of our inherent goodness as beloved children of the Loving Creator.

If you look inside, you will find the courage to face a delusion—a limiting or grandiose belief that may be holding you back from life. Ask for your perceptions to be clear, so that you can recognize an illusion in the way you view yourself or the world. With each breath, breathe in life. Then, as you breathe out, release the falseness that has bound you, and shake yourself gently free.

Let yourself see something familiar that you have never really seen before: a tree in your yard, a blade of grass, the color of a loved one's eyes, the textures of your own hand. Expand your capacity to receive reality and take pleasure in the act. As you take pleasure in the ordinary, your need for illusion and delusion will soon lessen and reality will bring sweetness to your world.

 Thou shalt not cling falsely to any other of thy delusions, nor to thy tedious disbeliefs, for safety or stubbornness' sake.

Feast 9

There is a difference between questioning and asking questions. Questioning strikes at the integrity of someone or something—as when a friend says, "Are you questioning my judgment?"

To ask a question, though, is to express interest, curiosity, and a desire to know. Questions always begin with words like *what, who, how, when, where,* and *why.* Relationships unfold as we ask questions and, thereby, indicate our willingness to know one another.

In his beautiful book, *Kinship with All Life,* J. Allen Boone describes entering into a deep and fulfilling friendship with a gifted German Shepherd named Strongheart who had performed in motion pictures years earlier. Boone's description of his evolving relationship with the dog reveals that he, in effect, learned to ask the dog questions.

When Strongheart first came to him, the human was inclined to treat the dog as an object, who by rote, was fed, walked, groomed, and trained. Within hours, the human realized that two living beings were encountering each other and that mutual adjustment, patience, and openness were essential to this meeting.

Soon Boone learned that if he watched the dog's behavior carefully, a whole new way of perceiving the world unfolded: two remarkable beings could share this world in a way that was pleasing to both. The dog's animal wisdom was revealed to the human because Boone became willing to learn by discovering a different mode of consciousness and by asking questions of that consciousness.

The two creatures learned one another's vocabulary and discovered ways of asking questions like, "What is the best route through this neighborhood? Where shall we rest and eat lunch? Will it rain soon? Is it nap time?"

Anyone who has ever shared emotional intimacy with a creature of another species will understand this. It is more than the affection that naturally evolves through mutual respect. It is also having surprising experiences together made possible by asking questions in trust and by responding in trust.

One day Boone wanted to take Strongheart on a walk through one of their usual routes in the city. The dog looked into Boone's eyes in a way that caught the man's attention, and Boone asked, "Where shall we go?" The dog led and the man followed, having by now become aware of the dog's remarkable wisdom. Soon they were climbing a hill. They reached the top as the sun began to set. Strongheart found the best spot to view the western sky and immediately settled himself and began to gaze in awe. His manner changed from the excitement of the shared climb to a meditative and deeply receptive serenity. The man followed the dog's example. Together they shared a moment of profound beauty and stillness. The right question had been asked.

Seek in yourself ways you are unsure of or don't know, and then find the liberating question that will bring the information you need. Ask it of someone you trust. And be willing to follow the answer to the next question, and the next, and the next. As questions lead to knowledge and to more questions, wisdom comes. Soon you will follow your wisdom to your own places of sunset and wonder. Soon you will follow wisdom home, home to your best self.

     Thou shalt not be afraid to ask questions.

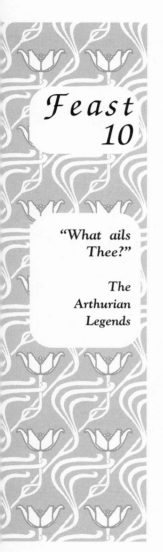

"What ails Thee?"

The Arthurian Legends

*T*he Arthurian Legends, by Wolfram von Eschenbach, is a German version of the story of the Holy Grail. In this legend, healing begins with a single question. The Grail King, the story goes, lived alone in his castle, suffering great anguish. He had been pierced by a poisoned spear, and the venom was such that he would not die, but rather be perpetually in pain from a wound that would not heal. The only way to break the evil spell of the venom was to say the right words. These words could only be in the form of a question.

A knight of the land, Parcifal, embarked on a journey, a holy quest. He faced a series of adventures—but with each adventure, he was required to ask the right question. When Parcifal failed to ask the essential first question, "Whom does the Grail serve?" he was told, "Thou didst cover thyself with sin, since thy fair-spoken mouth, alas, was mute, and did not question." But the knight was mercifully given another chance.

Many brave knights had already failed to bring relief to the wounded King because they did not understand that a simple direct question held the power to heal him. The question was to be asked spontaneously, without coaching, but with trust in one's natural human compassion and innocent impulse toward inquiry.

Each knight, in turn, failed to do what was called for: enter the castle, find the King, and ask the question that would heal the wound. One after another beheld the King's great affliction, yet did not ask his host: "Sir, what has caused your suffering?"

That question, of course, would have been an invitation for the King to tell his story, and to experience spiritual and emotional healing in the process of telling his truth to a caring witness. In telling the truth about his wound, the King—like us—could bring the pain outside himself and share it with another human being. Pain is lightened when it is shared, and by being shared, it becomes part of the story of all humanity.

Ultimately Parcifal asked the crucial question simply as, "What ails thee?" In these few words, an anguished inner world was opened to light. The deep wound was recognized, and the King could be healed, finally free from the pain that had kept him prisoner. Recognition is often enough to begin healing, but without it, healing can never begin.

We all have wounds whose curse it is to imprison us in pain because they cannot be shared. Only you know your wounds. Only you know the suffering you experience by keeping your anguish away from the eyes of those who love you. You may first need to ask yourself gently, "What ails me?"

To begin, breathe deeply, slowly, intentionally. Be still in yourself, and let yourself notice the wounded place inside. Observe it with openness, and simply recognize its need for healing. Then consider a way to find a trustworthy witness who will listen to your story with respect and compassion. Tell your truth to the witness when you feel ready to do so. Be patient with yourself and with your pain. Remember that the Creator is also your witness, the most loving witness you could have. Trust your truth. Finally, let healing begin as you ask the important questions.

 Thou shalt learn to ask the truly helpful questions and to live them patiently.

"*Because he believes in himself, he doesn't try to convince others. Because [s]he is content with [her]self, [s]he doesn't need others' approval.*"

Tao Te Ching

We can all become intensely devoted to being right, to having things our own way, and to defending our judgments and decisions. We can all perceive questions or attempts at negotiation from others as a threat to our power. We all hate, to varying degrees, to be found in error. Silly as it may seem, we are more apt to be unwilling to admit that we are wrong about the most trivial things. Harsh stares and protruding chins in heavy traffic, flared tempers during dinner arguments about place names or conflicting memories all reflect some hidden, unexpressed insecurity which manifests in the determination to be right. When we insist we are right, we become closed and uneducable. We become committed to ignorance and to having things our own way.

We must remind ourselves to be careful before committing to certainty. It is important to take enough time to be sure of ourselves before acting or speaking. Instead, it is all right to make tentative judgments, to sit with them, and to shift them around in order to determine which is truest. And it is all right to say, "No, this is not right after all. I was wrong. I need to let go and revise my perspective." It is all right to do this as many times as is necessary in order to choose and act in ways that feel the best.

It is even all right to stop midway and say, "What I am doing is wrong. I am in error. I am off track. Let me go back and begin again with greater attention, information, and care. Let me go more slowly and be more sure."

Sometimes it is wise to seek perspective and validation from others in order to avoid mistakes and possible damage. Fortunately, most situations in daily life require choices and actions that are not irreversible. So it is all right to approach life as an experiment—testing it and changing our decisions. It is all right to tell others what is happening, just as it is all right to preserve our privacy and keep the process internal.

Most of us are bombarded daily with more information than we can possibly absorb. As we become subject to information fatigue, our circuits overload, and our information retrieval systems burn out. Then we may feel completely sure of ourselves, yet be utterly wrong.

We have all proven our ability to deceive ourselves this way, and we know we need to stay open to more information and to correction. Not to stay open invites danger and risks placing others in danger as well. We need to know that it is all right to be wrong, as long as we are willing to admit it and to learn.

Scientists are a good example. When a scientist develops a theory, his or her job is to prove that theory correct. But every other scientist has the job of disproving it. If a theory is disproved, the originator is called upon to dismiss gracefully that "crazy notion." When someone else is inspired with another crazy notion, the whole process is repeated. In this way, human intellectual understanding evolves.

Make a commitment to yourself to be correctable. Let yourself abandon a fixed notion. Let life reeducate you. Because good learning is cause for joy, be willing to say with joy, "I was wrong." Be tolerant of yourself, and be tolerant of others as they struggle with their needs to be right and their attempts to allow life to reeducate them.

 Thou shalt remember that it is all right to be wrong, and to admit it.

Feast 12

"In her greatest strength she is overcome; in her blindness, she sees most clearly . . . The higher she soars, the more brightly she shines as the reflection of God."

Mechthild of Magdeburg (Thirteenth Century)

*T*he word *fool* originally referred to something inflated with air. There is a sweet and airy English dessert, for example, called a fool. From that definition, fool came to mean a windbag, all noise and no substance. However, it also came to mean a truly inspired being, light and taking to the air on wings of originality and grace. A fool can either be rash and egotistical, or innocent and brave. As an archetype, the fool symbolizes spiritual innocence and the sacred adventurer who dares beginnings with great optimism—a dreamer whose cosmic wisdom illuminates the difficult choices life presents.

The fool, to others, may seem overly confident, mindless of imminent dangers. However, the holy fool is not just ebullient, but enthused, inspired, and filled. When filled and inspired, any risk becomes possible, any journey a spiritual quest. These are the most positive aspects of the fool: someone who is sensitive but willing to be scoffed at for the sake of dedication to the call from the Holy One and from within. The fool, in this case, is a great adventurer—wise, discerning, and motivated by a greater good.

Sometimes outsiders are not sure which aspect of the fool they are seeing in us: the deluded, careless dreamer or the inspired seeker and risk-taker. That is when we are challenged to hold to our innocent courage, even if others think we are in folly. We are also wise, when questioned, to make an honest self-examination: Are we deluded and selfish, or genuinely inspired? Is the quest worthwhile, or are we simply jousting with windmills? This is where wisdom is truly necessary.

In Hebrew Wisdom literature, Wisdom is described as the feminine aspect of God. She is the spontaneous, loving, active power that guides and inspires. She is a faithful spirit, playful and illuminating. Through Wisdom, creativity gives birth to art, music, literature, adventure, and understanding.

In one Hebrew metaphor, Wisdom is called the playmate of God, but we can also think of it as the playfulness of God. Wisdom is like a mother who dances with her child in the sunlight; when Wisdom laughs, it is the sound of the pure, loving delight a mother takes in her beloved child.

When we respond to life with our best, most daring creativity, we are playing the fool for Wisdom's sake. We know that we risk failure, but, if failure comes, we can find the mercy and the power to forgive ourselves and move on. We may even find the grace to laugh at our folly and discover a new gentleness within.

In the light of sun or candle flame, open your arms as an innocent child and listen for the Wisdom that speaks lovingly from within. Be creative, and take the risks necessary to make something new or to start an adventure. Laugh with Wisdom: laugh at yourself, at your innocent folly, and laugh in delight at daring to be a fool.

 Thou shalt not be afraid to be foolish, for Wisdom loves the honest risk-taker, and thou shalt laugh gently with her.

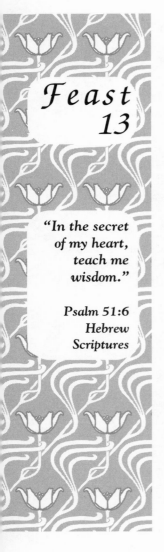

*"In the secret
of my heart,
teach me
wisdom."*

Psalm 51:6
Hebrew
Scriptures

I often ask God to help me learn from other people's mistakes. I sense that God's response is standard: "You know that you learn best from your own."

It is difficult for any of us to accept graciously as a gift from God the opportunity to learn from our mistakes. But if they can not at least be that, what possible good are mistakes?

If we choose to view them as gifts, mistakes can be daily opportunities for transformation of consciousness. On the occasion of mistakes, or as soon after as possible, we all need the grace to overcome our dullness, transcend our limitation, and, by the best means available, amend the effects of our errors. We need our lack of awareness healed, so that we do not fall into the familiar habit of failing to respond well to life's challenges. We need to remember to remain deeply alert to the opportunities presented by every occasion, even the occasion of mistake.

The gifted endocrinologist and healer, Deepak Chopra, suggests in his book, *Quantum Healing,* that physical illness may, in fact, be a failure of memory on the cellular level. Our cells, he believes, remember the wrong things—they literally remember and repeat their mistakes—and the result is that we become ill. Since every cell in the body is destined to begin dying nearly as soon as it is born, it cannot be said with accuracy that a tumor of a year ago is "still there." What is there is perhaps the hundredth reproduction of the original mistake in the body's growth process. The body simply kept doing the same wrong thing! The effect of an error in the smallest area can be all-pervasive. One thing can lead to six or six million others, because everything and everyone affects everything and everyone else.

To reverse the mechanism of a harmful process, we must reeducate at the point of origin. As in Chopra's paradigm of cellular memory, healing involves waking up the cells and shifting their attention from the repetition of their ongoing mistake to the correct model of health at the level of self-replication. This awakening and reeducation process can serve as a metaphor for how we can correct mistakes and harmful repetitions in our consciousness and behavior.

Errors can be seen as failures to be fully conscious or to pay full attention to our surroundings. Indeed, when we were children, our teachers often admonished us to, "Pay attention." As we come later in life to recognize that everything and everyone is a potential teacher, and as we learn to be increasingly alert and discerning through our lifetime, we can learn and repeat those things most in harmony with our own well-being and the well-being of the whole of which we are a vital part.

Gently strive to be aware of your participation in the larger life processes around you. Know that you are a significant, important part of the human family, of Earth's body, and of the cosmos. Realize that what you think, feel, and do has an effect on the life of the whole.

Intend well and attend well.

Act in harmony with what you perceive to be true. If you make a mistake, just let it go and make your amends. Have faith in the process and in your role in the process. And, finally, remember to give thanks for the opportunity to keep learning.

   Thou shalt not, however, keep doing the same dumb things without learning, with a humble and grateful heart, from the gift of thy mistakes.

> "The way
> (Tao) is
> called the
> Great Mother:
> empty yet
> inexhaustible,
> it gives birth
> to infinite
> worlds."
>
> *Tao Te Ching*

Rage almost always results from perceived injustices. We first perceive, accurately or inaccurately, injustices against ourselves. When we were young children, we could not discern between "I want," and "I need." What we wanted may not have been at all what we needed. Frustration of wants may have resulted in tantrums of rage.

The deprivation of true needs, like safety, touch, and basic care, can be so devastating to a child that the child does not respond in rage but is emotionally paralyzed. If the deprivation is significant enough, severe psychological and physical damage often result. As we grow up, remembering those occasions when the needy child was deprived or when wants were constantly frustrated, justified rage may come from our recognition of the harm perpetrated on us.

Few of us grow out of our childhoods unscathed, and most of us were at one time or another unprotected. Intentional, as well as accidental, harm may come to any child. For no matter how carefully adults attempt to protect children, none of us can guarantee a child's absolute safety. The world isn't a safe place, and each of us is vulnerable by simply being here.

As adults, we are responsible for helping the hurt child we may still carry inside to heal. Taking care of the inner child is always possible, for our present conscious self is never out of calling range to former selves carried now in our unconscious.

"Do we ever grow up, or get over being children?" someone asked recently. The answer was easy: "No. We carry all our ages inside us— from the newborn infant to the old man or old woman." The benefit of that inner cast of different-aged characters is that each of our ages has its own wisdom. In Hebrew Scripture it is written, "A little child shall lead them." Perhaps that is a metaphor for the mission of the healed inner child, the wise child in us all.

The archetype of the wise child is accessible to each of us. Sages can be any age, particularly when they live entirely in the spiritual dimension of our souls. These inner psychological figures wait to teach and guide us, but they need our humble attention. Our conscious adult attention is particularly needed in order to discern whether it is the healed wise child or the unhealed wounded child who is leading us.

We are all led by the child within, especially when we are under stress, or when the inner child is summoned by present-day events significantly similar to those of childhood. To the wounded child who may be responding with rage or paralysis, we may say, "I am aware of you. I promise to protect you and to listen to your pain."

If the wounded child needs to express anguish or rage, we need to give the child a safe time and place to do this so there can be a true release. Otherwise, we may be unconsciously controlled by the outraged wounded child within and behave in ways truly not connected to our present-day self.

Begin by finding a photograph of yourself at a young age. Frame it and put it in a special, visible place. Every day, spend a few minutes with the photograph, and open your heart and mind to the tender, vulnerable part of yourself it portrays. Listen to what that part of you is saying.

Meditate with your inner child. Create a loving atmosphere in your heart so that the wounded child within feels invited, welcomed, and protected in asking for healing. Imagine yourself taking this precious part of you into your arms. Invite it to become the wise child within and to tell you what else is needed. Let the wounded child and the wise child speak and listen to each other. The wise one will help you to heal the wounded one.

Together, they will teach you to be compassionate and responsive to your own needs and to those wise and wounded aspects of other fragile human beings. Breathe out residual rage on behalf of the wounded child, and breathe in blessing and acceptance.

Tending the Wounded Wild Child can free the Wise Wonder Child.

 *Thou shalt relinquish thy rage after
listening to thy hurt child within and learning
what thou needest to feel safe.*

Feast 15

"Come to my aid, O Holy One, for violence overpowers me, desecrates my integrity, blames me for its sin."

WomanWitness

We need not look further than the front section of the daily newspaper to find the faces of those who have experienced terrorism, natural disaster, or the ravages of injustice: victims of war, the homeless, the ill, the bereaved, the addicted, the wrongly accused. In our normal work and play, we may personally encounter others who also suffer from injustices by being ignored, neglected, or ridiculed—or by being made to feel invisible and worthless in our society. We often turn our heads and pass people by whose lives have been unjustly denied and who have been deprived of basic human dignity.

If we permit ourselves really to see the injustice and suffering around us, we are immediately challenged. How will we respond? Will we protect ourselves by numbing our emotions, ignoring the pain of others, and blinding ourselves to their needs? Will we be shattered by the realization of our own inadequacy in meeting the needs of others? Will we feel overwhelmed and retreat from reality? Will we despair because we are not able to respond in a meaningful way?

Each of us has a storehouse of potential energy that can be tapped and used to help change our world. We can begin by allowing ourselves to feel anger and indignation at our composite life experiences. Instead of pushing those emotions aside, we can experience their energy and focus on that energy for help.

Rather than throw up our hands in despair, we can recognize that even in the face of huge human suffering and overwhelming destruction to the planet, there are things each of us can do.

It counts to speak out when we hear someone expressing bigotry. It counts to refuse to remain silent in a meeting when prejudice manifests itself. Taking the time to write a concerned letter to one's congressional representatives about an important issue counts. Something as small as intervening between a bully bluejay and a hungry goldfinch at the feeder counts. In such ways, we express our convictions with care and join in the collective intention to work together toward the common good.

Try to focus your attention on your own gifts, those which might be put to use to make an improvement on Earth. Be realistic. Start small. Know that every act of kindness and courage anywhere counteracts inertia and evil everywhere. Make a conscious intentional offering each day toward the well-being of our corporate life.

Remember, smiling at a neighbor counts. Feeding the birds counts. Refraining from your own impulse to kill by showing a fly the way outside counts. Praising a laborer counts. Inquiring kindly about the cashier's day at the grocery store counts. Thanking a family member for an ordinary contribution to daily life counts. As a part of the human community, any positive act you make counts to improve life for us all.

 *Thou shalt focus and use thy righteous anger against injustice
to change reality for the greater well-being of all.*

Feast 16

"*Compared to light, [Wisdom] takes precedence; for that, indeed, night supplants, but wickedness prevails not over Wisdom.*"

Book of
Wisdom
7:30

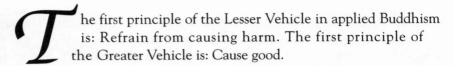

The first principle of the Lesser Vehicle in applied Buddhism is: Refrain from causing harm. The first principle of the Greater Vehicle is: Cause good.

The most basic method for contributing to the general well-being of all is to do no harm, to avoid injuring even the smallest creature as much as possible. Beyond this, it is a blessing to bring about greater well-being for all creatures, large and small.

A colloquial way of saying this would be, "If you can't help, at least stay out of the way." But, of course, everyone can help.

Begin with yourself. What is important to you? Then look around your own part of our world and see if you find evidence that what you value is what is being enacted. If children are important to you, do you see them well-treated in your community? If you love nature, look around and see if trees are planted or if land is kept in reserve for wildlife. Or if you value the arts, are there scholarships for young artists, a community theater, or musicians who get together to create beautiful sounds? If you don't see enacted what you value, get angry for the sake of good; raise hell for the sake of heaven.

Begin by recognizing what is important and what is needed. Proceed according to your own ability, and, remember, you are most effective when you focus on a specific object.

Let simplicity dictate limits. Don't get too complicated in your effort to change the world, or you will exhaust yourself and need to quit before you even begin to see results.

Whenever possible, try not to act alone. An individual alone cannot take the bold action sometimes required, nor absorb the social repercussion that may follow bold action. An individual is easily ignored, and tires too quickly to sustain what is usually needed to push for permanent improvement. Two slogans for effectiveness might be: "Keep it simple," and "Get help".

So go ahead and get angry about something that needs to be changed. Use that anger to give you energy to act effectively. Then find help and inspire others with your righteous anger. Organize. Form a committee. Delegate the responsibility. Forward march!

 Thou shalt raise hell, from time to time, for heaven's sake.

Feast 17

My father once said, "We know we're grown up when we're able to forgive our parents for being human." He was right in two ways: first, our parents, as we, are flawed human beings in need of forgiveness; second, forgiveness is a spiritual gift we grow into that is truly a mark of maturity. We cannot rush ourselves through the process of forgiveness, or we risk missing the understanding and wisdom that it gives.

Sometimes that wisdom comes from paradox. In trying to understand, accept, and then forgive someone, we may find ourselves in the midst of a situation that defies understanding and which cannot be acceptable under any terms.

Then what we must come to understand and accept is that we can neither understand, nor accept, what has happened. In that paradox, we experience our own human flaws, our own limitations, and, thereby, come to better understand the flaws of others.

From time to time, we all cause harm to others. Causing harm separates us from those we have injured and alienates us from our own best selves. In seeking forgiveness, however, we indicate we are ready to be reunited with our best selves and to be restored to right relationships with others. We want to rejoin, as members in good standing, the whole human family.

But we must accept acceptance. If we do not, in humility, forgive ourselves, our refusal remains a barrier between ourselves and others—a barrier within our own souls for future growth.

Forgiveness from others and forgiveness from self are two phases of a single breath: taking in new life and releasing old pains and resentments that stop the life flow. The humility to see that we need to forgive ourselves and others is freeing, because it reminds us again of who we are: human beings. This awareness is the basis for mutual tolerance, compassion, and forgiveness.

The possibility to do harm and to do good exists within each of us. Each of us is equally bound by the effects of the choices we make to do good or harm. No one is exempt from this reality of the human condition. So the need and the right to ask for forgiveness pertain to every child of God.

Consider how you feel about your place in the whole of humanity. Are your relationships with others comfortable and free of guilt and resentment? Do you have a relationship that needs healing through forgiveness? Are you ready to risk asking and receiving?

Look inside yourself, and find any barrier that might prohibit you from the process. Breathe into it, and imagine breaking through it. Imagine what needs to be said and done. Now what do you need to bring this image into reality? How can you become willing to give and to receive forgiveness for yourself and to offer forgiveness to others?

On the next page is the "Love Mantra for Letting Go." You may find this empowering as you prepare for forgiveness. Meditate on it as you picture others whom you need to forgive, or even yourself as the "you" in the prayer. Complete a full breath between each break in the text, inhaling on the first sentence in each part and exhaling on the second sentence. Read it slowly and consciously.

Love Mantra for Letting Go

I bless you,
I release you.

I set you free,
I set me free.

I let you be,
I let me be.

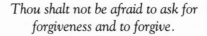

Thou shalt not be afraid to ask for
forgiveness and to forgive.

Feast 18

"Whatever
is true . . .
whatever is
just . . . if
there is any
excellence and
if there is any-
thing worthy
of praise;
think about
these things."

Philippians 4:8
New Testament

An observable fact of life is that human beings often see the obvious last and forget it first. The nearer something is to us, or the more immersed we are in a situation, the more likely it is that we will miss the obvious. Sometimes it is because of a lack of objectivity, as when a parent notices how tall her son is after he's been at camp for two weeks. Sometimes it has nothing to do with objectivity—we just don't see what is right there in front of us.

Anthropologists are familiar with the tendency to miss the obvious and know that expectation often limits and shapes perception. We sometimes don't see something simply because we don't expect to see it. The brain tends to pre-empt the eye or ear—and create reality based on past experience—before new information can penetrate. Many errors in judgment are caused by the replacement of reality with preconceived notions of what ought to be, rather than what really is.

A story is told in anthropological circles about the residents of a tropical shore who literally could not see a ship as it approached because they had never seen a ship. They had no frame of reference which would have made recognition of the ship possible. They literally saw nothing on the horizon. We do not see what we do not believe to be possible. Conversely, people who see the face of Elvis or Jesus superimposed on city billboards are seeing what they believe could be there. In the same way, children who see monsters in the corners of their rooms are seeing what they fear, and child-like adults who see ill-will in other people may do so because of past abuse, which is familiar and, therefore, expected.

Limited by expectations, past experience, or lack of frame of reference, we often fail to see what is. That is why we need each other, and why the differences among us are helpful. We need our friends with different sets of beliefs, fears, desires, and expectations to point out the obvious for us and to remind us of the obvious when we forget it.

Every time a guest comes to visit, I discover something about my own home that, because of familiarity, I didn't recognize before. It may be something as obvious as needing another shelf above the pile of books on the floor or an eye-strain problem that could be solved by using a higher-wattage light bulb. Or maybe, because of habit, I have forgotten I have the power to move the bench that is always in my way or to reposition a chair by the window to see the view outside more clearly.

Life is enriched when we remember that we know how to be efficient, that we can ask for help, and that we are creative. These are all realities so close to us that we become blind to them, or forget about them. We need to remember to keep looking and listening and, at the same time, to be willing to accept the invitation to move beyond fixed perceptions—to see and hear in new and deeper ways. The world becomes brand-new when we permit ourselves to meet it on its own terms.

Invite life to take you by surprise by showing you something that is obvious but something that you have habitually overlooked. Be open. Pretend that this is your first day here and that you are meeting everything and everyone for the first time. See with new eyes—the eyes of your wise heart.

 Thou shalt remember the obvious and not belabor it.

Feast 19

*P*ain and power are each other's shadow. Pain is nature's way of calling our attention to an underlying problem. To ignore pain is dangerous, because the wound from which it comes, if left untended, could bear destructive consequences to the whole being. If we recognize injury to our body or soul through physical or emotional pain, we are empowered to heal the wound and to restore ourselves to health and integrity.

If we forget, however, that pain is a symptom and not an absolute condition, we may give up our power and succumb to defeat too quickly. Rather, we need to move through any denial or despair about our pain and use our power and creativity to bring us into new awareness.

Pain is a call to attention; it brings the gift of awareness. In becoming aware that suffering is a feature of life experienced by all creatures, we can overcome the despair of feeling ourselves cut-off and alone, separate from other living things. Recognition of pain and injury in another person brings us comfort and reassurance; but more importantly, it brings us a chance to stay actively connected with others.

In the same way, animals, in their natural tenderness, can have a profound effect on us and on other animals. A friend of mine showed me a photograph of her burro at the veterinarian's office after he had been attacked by a wild dog. Another burro was also staying at the animal hospital, recovering from a less serious injury. Before my friend's burro died, the other burro befriended him and lovingly cared for him. In the photograph, I saw the less injured burro gently nuzzling him with an expression of infinite tenderness on her face. He was visibly soothed. Fear was nowhere present. The only emotion present was the peace-giving power of love, which all creatures can share.

In classical psychology, it is observed that the crisis emotions—fear, anger, sorrow, and shame—are balanced by the equally powerful emotions of interest and joy. All of these emotions are physiological links between the body and the mind. They communicate through the body what the mind perceives. They are signals or messages of our experiences, and they help us to decode our world, enabling us to respond to it appropriately. They are feelings that all animate beings have.

To be animate means to have the power of moving and of being moved by virtue of a soul: an essential, invisible, transcendent, expressive core. The Latin word for soul is anima. Notice that it is the root for animal, animate, and animation. Because we are animate—that is, because we can move and be moved—we are affected by life and by each other. We respond and we inspire response in others. We respond with feelings and with emotions. Emotions are feelings moving outward, feelings in motion.

Negative emotions are those we associate with pain. It is distressing to experience them. The so-called positive emotions are powerful enough to salve the painful emotions, even at the most primal, bodily level. The range of negative emotions may seem broader than that of the positive ones, but the positive emotions are astonishing in their effect, fully equal to all of the negative ones.

For example, feeling interest can counteract feeling anger, fear, or sorrow. Interest may seem odd in the context of feeling and emotion. We might consider it to be a kind of thought rather than a kind of feeling. Its power rests in the fact that it unites the thinking and feeling functions, and we know that deep interest leads to joy. The emotion of joy has countless nuances and expressions, ranging from tranquil serenity and contented pleasure to wild exuberance.

For example, people who are in great physical pain from certain advanced cancers and who are experiencing the accompanying grief and despair have reported that, beyond chemical medication, the one sure thing that helps is for them to become truly interested

in something. A friend said that only three things helped him to have relief from the acute, agonizing pain of a nerve disease: to ride his bicycle in the countryside, to visit his beautiful newborn twin granddaughters, and to think of his beloved. In these situations—when he was doing more than simply taking medicine—he became completely free of pain.

What happens is a shift in awareness. It is not just a matter of being distracted from the pain but of beginning to heal by finding real interest in something that we love.

Tears carry toxins out of the body as well as express pain or joy. The act of crying or laughing relaxes all the muscles of the upper body. It also permits the blood and the lymph system to flow more efficiently and do the healing work in the body. Giving ourselves permission to laugh or to cry is an expression of loving kindness toward ourselves. Laughing and crying are acts of freedom. They can help to heal what ails us and to unbind us from pain.

Just as all of us suffer, all of us have the power to make a healing shift in our attention and our attitude. We can let ourselves be taken out of pain and into the joy of something we love. It can be as basic as sunlight, music, chocolate pudding, flowers, or prayers.

Think about your pain honestly. What wound does it express? What gift does it offer you? How can you make use of the gift?

Remember your link with others. Compassion is willingness to share in the passion of others, without condemnation. But first, you must acknowledge your own passion and treat yourself with compassion by affirming—not running from—your own pain. Your power to feel your own emotions and the emotions of others is the power of life within you. Allow that power to flow into the world as a blessing.

Thou shalt not underestimate thy power nor minimalize thy pain, but learn to use both compassionately.

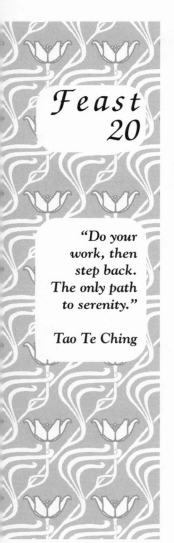

"Do your
work, then
step back.
The only path
to serenity."

Tao Te Ching

My grandma used to say, "Fret not thy gizzard." This is grandmother wisdom. She got it from her grandmother, who got it from her grandmother. It was meant to surprise a child into a smile or a giggle. But it can also remind the desolate soul that life changes, and tomorrow may bring joy as today brought sorrow.

In the inimitable words of Walt Kelly's wise possum hero, Pogo, "Don't take life too serious. It ain't nohow permanent." Or perhaps it was the gently prickly Porkypine who said that. No matter. All the swamp critters understood.

When we are in danger of worrying ourselves sick, we are doing to our bodies what a dog does to a bone: gnawing it out of existence. If humans had gizzards, serious fretting could put them out of existence. We manage to interfere with the health of some of the good parts we do have by trying to solve all our problems by ourselves, all alone, and all at once. We forget that we really can solve our problems—with help—one by one.

My image of Divine Wisdom is very similar to my image of my grandma: patient, large, open, consoling, confident in her no-nonsense common sense, honest, direct, earthy, simple, and funny. When I need wisdom, I sit in my grandma's rocking chair and imagine that I am sitting in the lap of Grandma Wisdom. I sit there to listen to the sacred stories of others, and if I am still and receptive, sometimes Grandma Wisdom herself whispers into my ear.

Remember the wise ones in your life, those people who have been Grandma and Grandpa Wisdom to you. Imagine them around you. Take a problem to them. Instead of worrying yourself sick, or out of existence, relax and listen. You, too, may hear the whisper in your ear of Wisdom's soft voice.

   Thou shalt fret not thy gizzard.

Feast 21

The tenets of most of the world's faith systems can be summarized: right relationships in life mean living with a humble and grateful heart. A humble heart is our life's center. It knows that its source is Earth—the holy ground of our being—and it knows that it is also filled with love from the Divine Spirit.

Christian mystics have expressed this unity of matter and spirit in the acknowledgment of God's presence dwelling in all beings in all creation. There is also a Talmudic image that serves as a charming metaphor for the same idea: every blade of grass has its own guardian angel, encouraging it to grow and be healthy.

In the most hideous conditions of human misery or in the wake of a terrible natural disaster, there remains the possibility of change. These conditions, no matter how awful, are not permanent. Life is a dynamic process. Everything is always moving, becoming, interacting with other beings in the divine dance played out in creation. For the dance itself, we can be grateful.

Gratitude is the joyful, accepting response to Grace, which means Gift; the gift of love bestowed in life itself. When we open our hearts in simple gratitude, we feel the deep joy of life and the natural flow of love in the soul. When we are grateful for a beautiful sunset, for sleep, for the beginning of a new life each morning, we experience the wholeness of life within and beyond ourselves. We are in harmony with what happens and that is happiness. One cannot be in harmony with suffering or with evil, for they are discords in nature, necessary, but chaotic and defying comprehension. Despite suffering and evil, we can still seek the essential goodness and integrity at the core of existence and trust in them ultimately to triumph over evil.

Happiness is not a habit, but a skill. It takes practice. We must have the daily intention to live with a humble and grateful heart and be in harmony with what life brings us in order to be truly happy.

An ancient Spanish hymn begins, "My God, I love thee; not because I hope for heaven thereby, Nor yet for fear that loving not I might forever die." The song's translator continues to develop the theme that the soul loves because it is naturally drawn to love, and in the joy of loving and expressing gratitude, one loves freely. A similar belief was expressed by a Sufi poet, who wrote the following passage:

"God, if I love you in order to avoid hell, may I go to hell. If I love you in order to attain heaven, may heaven close its door to me. But if I love solely for Your own sake—then, Beloved, show to me thy face."

Practice happiness in your life each day. Take your practice of happiness outdoors and delight in the sustaining air around you, in the light, and in the day. Sing a song of joy. Be glad another day is beginning. Use each day to create harmony somewhere. Write a thank-you note to God, or to another loved one or to yourself. Celebrate what comes your way.

Thou shalt not forget to celebrate and practice happiness
and breathe in and out with a grateful heart every day for all
God's gifts to thee and in thee.

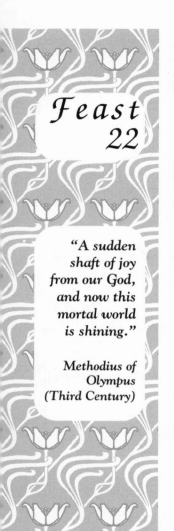

"A sudden
shaft of joy
from our God,
and now this
mortal world
is shining."

Methodius of
Olympus
(Third Century)

Ancient prayers of thanksgiving recognize all of creation as the Body of God, an outward and visible sign of the presence of the Great One, the Source, the Mother of the Cosmos.

If we recognize that creation is holy, and that it is a gift, it becomes impossible to mistreat any part of it. The environment is not some abstract thing outside ourselves; rather, it is the creative expression of God. Earth is not just our home, it is not just where we are, it is who we are. It is intimate and sacred to our lives.

Our need for survival is one with our need to protect what is sacred—the Earth who gives and sustains life. Mother Earth is an expression of Divine mother love. As Earth is to us, God is to Earth and to all cosmos. If Earth dies, we die. She is we. We cannot kill God, but we can kill God's gift; the Earth in whose sacred embrace we live.

The global movement toward caring for the Earth and repairing the harm our young species has caused her is an urgent awakening of our collective human consciousness (and our collective conscience) in the direction of making amends for our drunken misuse of life's gifts to us. Globally, we are experiencing individual and corporate awakening of our desire to help, the impulse to meet the needs of the beloved Earth entrusted to our care. This awakening is not a demand to follow rules or to obey restraints, but it is a call to express responsibility, the response-ability that is in each person's power. Our response evokes and quickens life in all of us.

As we respond in gratitude and come to the aid of our ailing Earth Mother, the energy we need comes from re-awakening our sense of wonder. If we have a sixth sense of intuition beyond the five senses of our bodies, we also have a seventh sense, the sense of wonder. This seventh sense is the one that opens us to discover more about our universe and what we mean here. Through wonder, we rekindle the joy of being here. Through wonder, we weave healing into the world and devote our passions and power to that great purpose. Through wonder, we show by our actions that we know we belong, and we will return Earth's welcome with deep respect and care.

So plan an Earth party. Look at the world in wonder and renew your covenant to care for the Earth. Where others are not yet aware that we have used our Mother Earth's body as a garbage dump, offer Earth a touch of kindness by cleaning the disrespect off her body. Have an Earth celebration with someone by sharing a communion of flowers and eating her fruit together, very slowly, in an attitude of prayer and gratitude.

*Thou shalt remember to take long walks out of doors
and to listen to the birds and smell the flowers and trees and to
touch the Earth and sing to her, and to have picnics
whenever possible.*

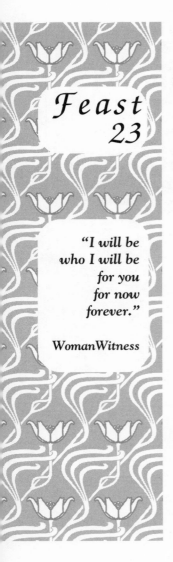

"I will be
who I will be
for you
for now
forever."

WomanWitness

*A*ll of our language that relates to the truly important, to what theologian Paul Tillich called matters of "ultimate concern," is metaphoric. Because we cannot define the indefinable, describe the indescribable, or limit the infinite, we can only say about those things that they are *as if*. When we say something is *as if*, we are using a metaphor. If we forget that we are speaking metaphorically, and our *as if* becomes *is*, we have slipped into glorifying our *idea* of what is instead of *what truly is*.

Every religious system has its own metaphors to describe the indescribable or the infinite. Even people who consider themselves nonreligious often recognize inner inclinations toward feelings of wonder, awe, gratitude, and love that defy exact definition. As modern physics tells us, we cannot even define all that composes the visible world, because even that is fluid, and, therefore, indefinable. The invisible world of feelings and values eludes definition. But we need to define and name reality enough to talk about it and to work with it. So we use a metaphor to talk about elusive things, those things experienced at the level of feeling, intuiting, or longing.

We have rich possibilities when we use metaphors and symbols to speak of our insights into the invisible Presence. In Tantra Yoga, the central metaphor is the marriage of Shakti and Shiva. Creative potential is symbolized by the male lover, Shiva, who dances in a circle of fire, representing the unbroken cyclical union of death and life, destruction and creation, chaos and order. Shakti, the female lover, is the symbol for the actualization of the creative potential. She is the divine mother love that gives birth to all that exists by bringing the circle of fire into the visible universe. The words *Tantra Yoga* themselves mean weaving and joining together. And as the divine feminine and masculine principles join together, their loving union weaves spirit into matter, being into life, and the Divine into the human. This same metaphor is used in Jewish mystical theology. It is celebrated every sabbath when human beings are blessed by symbolic participation in the divine lovemaking between the masculine and feminine aspects of the Creator. Further, in Hebrew Scripture—the basis for the three religious systems dominant in the West—metaphors for God include Mother, Friend, Companion, Light, Darkness, Fire, Mountain, Hand, Lover, Husband, Bride, Womb, Matrix, Eye, and Living Water. The Christian tradition adds images of Child and Father to the list of Hebrew names for God.

Native American and ancient Arabic religions alike use the metaphor of Essence or Mystery to describe what we call God. The word, translated from many Native American languages into English as "Great Spirit," would be more accurately given as Great Mystery, or Essence, as would the Arabic word *Allah*.

Modern spiritual metaphors for the Great Mystery include Higher Power and Inner Wisdom, showing that what we experience is both beyond and within. Metaphor is our way of talking about the unknown qualities and richness of something we sense by using the language of what we know and the images with which we are familiar. Metaphor is our only valid religious language and the natural language of the soul.

Recognize and think about your personal metaphors for that Presence you sense guiding you through life. Identify ways in which you speak about the Presence. Have any of your metaphors become meaningless, damaging, or too limiting because you have fallen into using them too literally? Loosen them up. Expand them. Vary them. Breathe freshness into your relationship with the precious, boundless, loving Presence you sense within you and beyond you. Keep it clear. Keep it simple.

 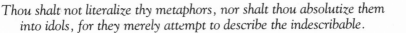

Thou shalt not literalize thy metaphors, nor shalt thou absolutize them into idols, for they merely attempt to describe the indescribable.

> *"Life is what happens while you're busy making other plans."*
>
> *John Lennon (1940–1980)*

*L*ife does things to us. It has its way with us. Everybody gets broken, one way or another. Our western pride, or hubris, ill-prepares us for this humbling reality, and we often respond in disgust, rejecting and berating ourselves for being weak, vulnerable, or failing to stand imperviously against the assaults of existence.

Thus begins a deadly cycle of self-hatred and self-deception. The frightened child within believes that bad things happen because we deserve them, or worse, that it is our own fault that they happen. Being abused or neglected is never a child's fault. But children believe themselves to be the center of the universe and assume that everything is their fault. When something bad happens the child inside believes he or she somehow made it happen. The damage deepens if we grow up without changing this wrong belief, and we continue to feel overly-responsible, not only for the pain in our own lives, but for all the pain in the world.

The situation worsens when we also use our self-hatred to treat others in pain with contempt. Vague guilt from over-responsibility and contempt of others combine, and the result can be confusion. This is the confusion of the wounded, untended child that may lie within any of us. Out of excessive, unrealistic guilt, we may try to use our power to change others in an attempt to fill the starved and empty ego inside.

Healing begins when we give the child its due. As adults, we can assume a nurturing role for our own inner child and treat that part of ourselves with care, patience, and tender acceptance. At the same time, we can reassure the wounded child that it was not responsible for the bad things that happened earlier in life.

As we release responsibility where we have assumed too much, we can freely accept responsibility where it is truly ours. In doing this, we need to have mercy toward the wounded child within; mercy toward our own slowness, weariness, and impatience; and mercy toward the many manifestations of brokenness in others. No blame, no shame. Our fragile souls are vulnerable to forces larger than ourselves.

Let yourself be aware that everyone around you has been battered by life in some way, whether it shows or not. Practice mercy with yourself and with others. Evaluate reality, and trust your own inner needs and wisdom. Let yourself feel safe before you commit yourself, and give others that opportunity also. Above all, never use a wound as a weapon.

 Thou shalt not hold thy brokenness against thyself,
nor others' against themselves.

Feast 25

*I*n this age of computer consciousness and the complex structures of civilization, it is sometimes difficult to touch the Earth and to remember the part in each of us which is uncivilized and a bit wild.

When we use the word *wild* to describe human behavior, we usually refer to someone who is out of control, behaving in a chaotic way, or expressing energy unpredictably. We may mean that the person is out of reach because we do not know how to react to the wildness or how to tame it.

To tame a creature is to bring it under control by making it dependent. A wild animal that has been domesticated, brought into a human domicile, and made dependent, has been robbed of its innate power to sustain itself. It forgets what it is. We often say of wild animals we keep as pets that they think they are human. And we know that if they were returned to their own natural habitat, they would be helpless to hunt or to defend themselves. They would have forgotten how to act naturally and forgotten how to bring themselves into confident harmony with the rest of nature.

We have tamed ourselves. When human beings behave antisocially, they are not being wild; they are simply not bringing themselves into harmony with the rest of nature. They are acting out of control. They are acting out of even their own control. They are neither tame (receptive to the influence and help of others) nor wild, in harmony with nature. They are just lost.

To go to that natural wild place that is still within each of us and to express it freely, we need to play. We call adult play-time *recreation*, which really means re-creation. We recreate ourselves through the expression of our natural playfulness. From the natural place within, comes playfulness, a way of engaging in activity for the sheer pleasure of it, with pleasure being its only goal.

Our fiercely competitive sports of today have lost their playful quality because they are completely goal-oriented. The only goal is to win; the only purpose is to prove some kind of prowess. If we want to remember how to play, we can remember by watching other species of animals. They are usually experts at engaging in something, or nothing, for its own sake or for the sheer pleasure of it.

The most recreative times for humans are often those spent in actual wilderness: a summer camping trip, a canoe trip, a mountain hike, a nature walk, or even a lazy afternoon in the backyard with the birds. Any contact with Mother Earth will help us. As long as the backyard is blessed with growing things, it will serve.

In the middle of my back yard, there is a wild garden. It began as a wildflower garden, but over the years it has come to define itself, and it is now a wild garden. Weeds are welcomed there. What the garden wants to do, it does. Occasionally I turn the humus and give it a fresh start with a few seeds, but then nature resumes its authority and continues on its own terms. And that is my intent for it.

Around this garden is grass, which is regularly mowed, and small fruit trees, which are annually pruned. There are flower beds where weeds are not welcomed. There is even concrete, which is occasionally swept and scrubbed of moss. But the wild garden has little interference. It is vital to me that there is, in the center of my immediate world, a place allowed to be wild, a place that is tended and cared for, but not cultivated, not bent to human will.

When I look at my wonderful wild garden, I remember that equally wonderful wild place inside of me—the free and naturally creative place in my own soul. The wild garden helps me play and take time to gaze simply, to inhale Earth's sweet fragrances, and to admire the

strength and beauty of the creatures it is home to, both flora and fauna. The wild garden reminds me of why I am here: for the sheer pleasure and joy of being alive.

We may cultivate our manners toward the outside world, keep our intimate relationships well-weeded and free of emotional debris and slippery surfaces; but inside, oh inside, let there remain a place where even we can be surprised by what beauty and strength there is below our skin, waiting to spring forth and bring delight.

This is wildness. It is not antisocial. It is not defeated. It is the wildness of ancient forests and the wildness of the most fragile flower, the wildness of the sleek-furred ones, and of those who take wing. It is the wildness of the burrowing creatures who give air in the Earth below for the seeds to break open and grow. It is in you and in me. But we must provide a place for it. We must guard and protect that place.

Contemplate your own inner wild garden. How does your garden grow? What help can you give it? If it is only now but a dream, consider making a place for it. An Earth garden may help. Visit one that is not too tame or plant one for yourself. There are gardens in the imagination, too. Those you can always visit.

 Thou shalt be creative and playful in thine own special idiom, and delight thy Creator with thine ingenuity, which comes naturally and needs little cultivation.

*"[The wise
person]
holds nothing
back from life
and is there-
fore ready for
death."*

Stephen Mitchell
"Notes"
Tao Te Ching

*I*n Islamic wisdom, it is said that anyone who pollutes the Earth or her waters is an infidel. An act against creation is viewed as an act against the Creator. The face of the Creator shines forth in the face of all creatures. Even those creatures we do not like, or with which we have a natural incompatibility, reflect the features of the divine design. They, too, are children of God, and they, too, belong here.

Sometimes I think there is no good reason for certain things—mosquitoes, for instance. But that assumption on my part is due to my reluctance to be a part of the food chain, to be their dinner while I am still using my blood. If I could be unselfish, I would see that mosquitoes do fill an important need. They feed the birds, whom I would never begrudge; and the birds, or their close cousins, in turn, feed me and my kin.

All creatures nourish one another in various ways in our various places in the body of Earth. What is lost in one place always turns up in another. In the English translation of the words of Rilke, "Everything that happens keeps on being a beginning." This is a process we can trust.

To the carnivorous bird, the mosquito is a gift. It is a grace, and it is probably delicious. From the limited perspective of my species, I must suspend disbelief and accept this. Making the small sacrifice of my blood is cooperating with God's need to feed the birds. I cannot yet transcend my point of view far enough to consider that the mosquito might find its existence justified simply by living. It is challenging to accept that it also may take joy in being itself, and not just some other creature's dinner.

The wonderful thing about life is that nothing is wasted. Ultimately, all losses are redeemed and are rewoven into the total fabric; they are then made part of the wholeness and the holiness of being. This includes lost youth, lost health, and lost love. Healing always happens in the very big picture. That is the miracle of redemption: the bird released that returns to rest on your hand, or the child released from home that returns with your grandchild. And it is a gift.

Gifts are grace, and Grace is a gift. The many definitions of grace include gift, mercy, reconciliation, beauty, good will, kindness, unconditional love, moral strength, gratitude, and blessing before food. Its Greek root means to rejoice, and its Gaelic means to love. The original English root means to yearn.

Think about the gifts—the Grace that has appeared in your life. Think about how your life has already shown you that it is trustworthy. Life is love, and troubles are just a part of love. But the essence of love is fulfillment. That is the heart's desire.

Your life yearns for your trust and your joy. Even in the smallest thing, there is a basis for your trust. Even in the smallest events, there is Grace and there are gifts; abundant gifts you need simply to recognize, and trust they will always be there in one form or another.

     Thou shalt trust in God in thee and in all creatures,
for the possibility of redemption is boundless, and Grace is
everywhere accessible.

Feast 27

The Indian poet Tagore wrote, "God respects me when I work, but God loves me when I sing." Life is an experiment conducted by each of us. Life entrusts us with the opportunity to learn from our experiments. In the life laboratory, we are given what we need to meet each challenge and to embrace each lesson. Life has faith in us, and we can have faith in life. The German poet Goethe said, "As soon as you trust yourself, you will know how to live."

We live our faith and show our trust for life in the choices we make. The themes of our lives emerge from what we do, from what we love, and from how we love. Work and play can both be an expression of love. They can express our trust in life.

Sometimes we get in our own way. We block the free experiment of life because of fear that stems from our prejudicices or from our preconceived notions of how things should be.

We can be stubbornly resistant to a life lesson by refusing to be flexible in our methods. In striving for serenity, for example, we can refuse to participate in genuine and valuable conflict because it seems to contradict serenity. Conflict, however, may hold an important lesson whose gift we reject in our rigidity. Sooner or later, we will see that conflict is unavoidable because it disrupts our serenity in the form of anxiety or obsession.

Then we must revise our thinking and allow a more open understanding of what serenity might be. Only for babies does serenity mean the tranquillity of slumber. As adults, we cannot sedate ourselves and sleepwalk through life. Serenity means willingness to move confidently through conflict and to learn from it.

Review what you do, ways you love, and how you express that love. Is there some area where you are holding back because of fear or because you do not trust yourself or others? What hurt might be the basis for the mistrust? How have things changed? Talk to yourself about this. Ask for someone else's perspective. Believe that you can trust life to give you what you need.

 Thou shalt trust in thy Self as God trusts in thee, to fulfill thy destiny and to live thine experiment with life lovingly.

> "Keep on doing the things you have learned and received and heard and seen in me, and the God of Peace will be with you."
>
> Philippians 4:89
> New Testament

Children who did not attach to or bond with significant care givers suffer terribly and are painfully rigid. If they are not emotionally welcomed into the world, cared for, touched, talked to with tenderness, or intellectually stimulated during their first year of life, they will indeed suffer later. Whether their plight was caused by the physical death of their parents or by their parents' emotional absence, the result remains the same. When intimate and trustworthy love is unknown, great emotional suffering follows.

What we all needed as soon as we entered the world was the assurance that we would be cared for and loved. When a loving adult holds a baby, makes eye contact with it, smiles, talks, and coos with it, and treats it with sincere respect, the baby gets the message that it is loved and lovable. The child learns to view adults as trustworthy and the world as a safe place to explore.

When we, as babies, looked into our parents' wonder-filled eyes and saw ourselves mirrored back lovingly, we began to receive a sense of our own dignity and value. Babies deprived of this loving mirror for any reason—whether they are abused or not—do not properly develop emotionally or socially. They are always deficient in their ability to receive love and to trust others. They simply cannot recognize love when it is offered. They believe they are unprotected in an unsafe world. They respond to everything with mistrust, suspicion, and hostility. When they are picked up, they turn their heads away and arch their backs to make themselves untouchable. Any approach is perceived as potentially threatening.

Because they lacked loving contact when they first arrived, they do not feel attached or anchored in life through any bond of love. They may grow up to be "problem children" and later, even criminals. Without care, they could not form a conscience; therefore, they have no imaginative or emotional power for empathy. They exist in an isolated universe in which they alone are real, and their survival is all that counts.

The little baby we once were is still inside each of us. It still needs tenderness, welcoming reassurance, and loving respect. When we do not receive these things, we, too, can become rigid, withdrawn, and hostile. We continue to need daily assurances that we are loved and lovable. We never outgrow our need for kindness and tenderness.

When the Dalai Lama recently spoke at a conference on Spirit and Nature, he reminded us that the need for kindness and tenderness is shared by all living beings. While it may not be our present job to show tender mirroring to an infant, it is our job to show kindness and respect to all others as consistently as we can. He explained what he calls *spiritual democracy*, a universal respect for the unfolding spiritual destiny of others and an attitude of respectfully letting the spiritual journey of others simply be. Such an attitude comes from a deep trust that Life is guiding us as it is guiding others. Spiritual democracy also calls for a fundamental respect for our own and others' own unfolding destiny and mystery. It is ripe with affection and good will.

A respectful and wise person may weep more often than others for the sufferings of all beings, but she or he will also be quick with gentle laughter for the pleasures of the life we share. If God weeps cosmic tears over the suffering of creatures, there is sure to be a cosmic giggle at our pleasures. Both responses are expressions of divine tenderness, and each of us can open our hearts to that gift. Tenderness comes from genuine affection—from the willingness to respond to one another in well-wishing appreciation and warmth. The Dalai Lama encouraged each of his listeners to learn these skills—as he put it, to "learn the good heart. Of all things, the good heart is most precious."

Practice tenderness toward your own humanity. Do something tender for yourself, for another human being, and for a being who is a member of another species. Live into and

through your good heart. Pay attention to the possibilities for affection and loving tenderness this gives you.

Let respect be the basis of acceptance, and acceptance be the basis of affection, admiration, and appreciation. Extend these gifts to a tree or a flower and to a human being who is close to you.

 Thou shalt be tenderly kind to thy Self and to Others.

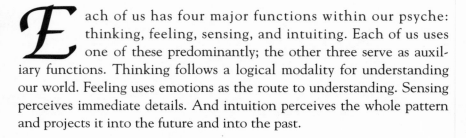

Feast 29

*E*ach of us has four major functions within our psyche: thinking, feeling, sensing, and intuiting. Each of us uses one of these predominantly; the other three serve as auxiliary functions. Thinking follows a logical modality for understanding our world. Feeling uses emotions as the route to understanding. Sensing perceives immediate details. And intuition perceives the whole pattern and projects it into the future and into the past.

The ideal solution is to integrate all these functions. Dysfunction and distortion arise when any of them is purposefully disowned or ignored.

In developing an auxiliary function more fully, we may lean toward the extreme. In coming to our senses, we may lose our minds. In thinking through a problem, we may lose heart. In minding our own business, we may lose a sense of others. In trusting our intuition, we may forget to be sensible. Any of these functions, when isolated from the others, can lead to trouble. Taken together, however, they help us to live in wholeness.

We have these four functions latent within us from the beginning. They need to be recognized, nurtured, and developed for us to live as whole beings fully present in our bodies and souls with open hearts and open minds. If the functions are in balance, we are in balance as the natural flow of life inside us is fostered. When we get out of balance by living too much in any one of them or by ignoring any of them, we may experience a block of the natural flow within our lives. Intentionally reaching out for help from trusted friends or professionals can be a way of restoring the flow and regaining balance.

True, we are each other's helpers, but all healing is really Self-healing; that is, each of us is gifted with the means to live in health and wholeness as a part of our nature. Help may come from the outside, but healing happens within.

The balance between inner resources and outer help, and the balance among the various functions, is dynamic. It is not a perfect balance; it is ever-changing. It is like the balance we have when we are walking—a balance achieved by always having one foot off the ground. It is a balance of rhythm, of movement, rather than one of stasis and weightedness. The ability to know these things instinctively is one of life's primary gifts.

Imagine yourself as part of a circle comprised of a variety of wise human beings and radiant celestial beings who will help you find your balance and keep your inner rivers of light flowing. Remember all your abilities, functions, and powers. Be open to helping others remember theirs also. Give thanks for your gifts. Keep giving thanks.

Thou shalt remember to rejoice in thine intellect, senses,
and holy emotions, and to make mutually beneficial contact with all
holy creation through them, relying always on thy creative power to
heal thy Self from within, which is God's
birth gift to thee.

*"For Wisdom
is a breath
of the power
of God, and a
pure emana-
tion of the
glory of the
Almighty."*

*Book of
Wisdom
7:25*

A Native American holy woman tells of her old, wise grandmother who cared for her family and imparted her wisdom and beliefs to them. When a corporation offered the wise old woman money for her land—trying to convince her of how her family would benefit from sudden riches—she responded, "We are already rich. We are rich because the land feeds us so well with good crops, and the waters give us such good fish."

The grandmother understood that true wealth comes from our common dependence on each other—our interdependence—and from the good life that abundantly flows forth from Nature. Each living being finds fulfillment through willingness to unfold as a vital expression of Nature and of the Divine.

Spirit is the life force within Nature, and Nature is home to Spirit. In the created universe, they are inseparable. In this living link of Spirit and Nature—which each of us is and in which we all live—each of us depends on others as we take our unique, individual place in the whole.

As we harmonize our personal dreams with the dream of the universe and with the dream of God, we are empowered to make our dreams come true. We have this right. It is our calling. Each of us has a unique contribution to make to the life of the cosmos, and we need the love and support of other dreamers to bring our unique contributions to the whole. With our willingness, Divine reality can be born in us and move through us. When we are willing, confidence will come, and the way will unfold. Healing and living will become one. All brokenness will be enfolded back into the fabric of wholeness. The process will continue. We can trust it.

Search your heart for its deepest desire, its most cherished dream. What help do you need to fulfill that desire and to bring the dream to reality? Are you willing to seek and to find what you need? Are you willing for God's face to shine through your life?

Thou shalt remember to ask for help in thy healing, and
thou shalt not be afraid to fulfill thy heart's desire, and thou shalt
in all things be willing for the Divine reality to be born in
thee and to move through thee, forever.

"Life, celebrate life. . . lighthearted light that enlightens the whole of us."

WomanWitness

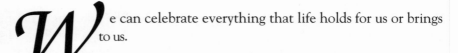 e can celebrate everything that life holds for us or brings to us.

Even pain, for it shows us our commonality with all other creatures.
Even depression, for it shows us our limits and helps us focus on healing.
Even despair, for it invites us to begin again with a single action.
Even death, for it is not what it appears to be; it is not an end, but a beginning which we barely understand in life.
Even human weakness, for it challenges us to make better choices beyond ourselves.

Dance your despair.
Cry your prayer.
Move in your depression.
Let pain teach compassion.
Let death teach hope.
Embrace weakness and let it become strength.

In this moment, let life begin.

 Celebrate everything.

Desserts for after the Feast

May the six poems that follow leave a sweet taste in your soul.
May they bless your place at the Feast of Life.

Be

Reality is intricate and vast.
You are real.
Life is cosmically generous.
You are gifted, alive.
The Universe holds.
You are embraced,
you belong.
It is enough.
You are enough.
Do not be centered in
yourself or the world,
but be a Self, centered in God.
Love and let Love.
Listen—Life is in love
with you!
Your life longs for
your trust.
Your life holds
and graciously
carries you through.
Every breath is an act
of faith and courage.
Your body believes.
Breathe.
Be inspired and let go.
Be faithful.
Be brave.
Be.

Three Little Words

If you want to be wise,
practice growing wonder-full.
Open your heart-mind
to the unknowable nature
of Nature, including yourself.
Consider yourself happy
to be a grain of sand
on the cosmic beach,
necessary for your part
and that is all.
Get comfortable with all
the possibilities that can
occur when you speak the truth
of these three words:
I don't know.
Embrace the insecurity of mystery
and its faithfulness also.
Fall in love with
the wonder of not-knowing.
Fill yourself with it.
Then breathe out your blessing
into the world
with a smiling heart.

What Jesus Really Said

Not much.

I am
here
now
with you.
I see you,
God-in-you.
I need to touch you.
I need you to touch me.
I need to be alone.
I will not leave you alone.

Respect all beings.
Be compassionate.
Take risks to help others
and to become your whole
self.
Be present in every moment.
Love as fully as life allows.
Live as fully as love allows.
I love you.

Let yourself be loved.
Accept acceptance.

Remember me.

The Tao of Christ
or Crazy Wisdom

"God has no religion."
—Gandhi

Being is the Way the Truth
and the Life.
Everything happens in the middle
of itself.
Ends happen in the middle. Also beginnings.
Then everything changes
again.
Be there always
in the middle
of things
and awake.
Read the times
for change.
If you can't read, sing.
If you can't sing, whistle.
If you don't know the language, dance.
Belong to God as God belongs
to all.
Above all, let your heart beat
thankfully.

with thanks to Wes "Scoop"
Nisker and his *Crazy Wisdom*

Buddha, Which Means Awakened One—
or, If You Meet the Buddha on the Road, Kiss Her

Did you know, Friend,
—the Earthpoet said—
all being is Buddhahood
and this means in bud?

Waking up the garden,
waking up the loam,
waking up the water,
waking up the stone—

Oh, do wake up—
wake up your eye
from its dream
and see how
nothing is better
than here, this, now—

this night-blessed morning.
Wake up by calling and hearing
each being's true name,
including your own,
and let the budding begin!

Listen—

There is no difference between
healing your body and healing the Earth
or helping another to heal.
It is all the same Body.

There is no difference between
healing Earth's body and healing your own
or helping another to heal.
We are all the One Body.

Begin anywhere.
Begin with one tree,
or a bird.
Begin with your own heart
or skin, clean out your liver,
clear your mind.
Begin with the growth of a child,
your family's food.
Then continue to include
one small part at a time.
You will be healing the Whole.

An Excerpt from
Life Is Goodbye, Life Is Hello:
Grieving Well Through All Kinds of Loss
by Rev. Alla Renée Bozarth, Ph.D.

Four Styles of Grieving

You and I are unique individuals. We respond differently to the same set of circumstances. Different people and different things hold different meanings for each of us. And yet we are similar in many ways. We share a common human nature. We are physical, spiritual, emotional, and intellectual in our make-up. We are both strong (in different ways). We share an ability to communicate, though our communicating styles may be quite different.

If both of us were faced with an identical loss—the loss of a job, for instance—our response might be surprisingly different, or strangely similar. Your initial response might be an optimistic assurance that you can go out and get any new job you want. My response might be to imagine myself destitute twenty years from now! Or we both might be crushed for a day or two, and then begin to explore new possibilities with confidence and determination. How we do respond to the situation of a grievous loss will depend largely on our own basic temperament and the effect that the sum of our separate experiences has had on each of us.

In my observation of the grieving process, four distinct styles of grieving have become recognizable to me. Despite our differences—the constitutional uniqueness of each of us—our common human nature will probably incline us toward one general grieving attitude or style should we find ourselves confronted with painful loss. We may take the attitude of the Hero, the Martyr, the Crazyperson, or the Fool. We may shift from one style to another, going through all four styles as we complete our process, or alternating between a combination of any two of them. Or we remain consistently with one grieving style, changing and growing according to the mode of that particular figure. Each of the four styles has a negative and a positive phase.

It may be helpful to consider both aspects of each figure or style in order to understand them more clearly. It may also be helpful to remember the four feeling stages – fear, guilt, rage, and sadness – common to those who grieve. These stages come *in between* the shock of loss and the renewed well-being which follows the healing process of realization. First, in severe loss which is the same as severe injury, there is shock – numbness, non-feeling; then feelings emerge, first in confusion, and gradually as distinct, clear emotional states that may succeed one another in any order, or may overlap and occasionally be felt simultaneously again. Through allowing oneself to experience these feelings and to integrate them fully with the rest of one's being, pain is gradually released and the ability to live life is regained. Well-being is restored.

For most people, then, the grieving process progresses like this:

> Shock
> four feeling stages: fear, guilt, rage, sadness
> well-being

It is in the feeling stages of this process that the four styles of grieving become apparent. The relationship of these grieving styles to the four corresponding feeling stages will become clear as we examine each style in its negative and positive aspects. Each style offers a way of individual development through the experience of loss, and no style is "better" than any other. The styles are simply different, each one better suited to a particular person at a particular time – and even then, with great room for variation within each style. They are simply ways of generalizing in order to understand and have confidence in the process.

Get your copy of **Life Is Goodbye/Life Is Hello:** *Grieving Well Through All Kinds of Loss* at your local bookstore, by using the order form on the next page, or by calling CompCare Publishers toll free at 1-800-328-3330.

Other Books From Compcare Publishers

Life Is Goodbye/Life Is Hello:
Grieving Well Through All Kinds of Loss
by Alla Renée Bozarth, Ph.D
ISBN 0-89638-115-3

A Journey Through Grief–Audio
Gentle, Specific Help to Get You through the Most Difficult Stages of Grieving
by Alla Renée Bozarth, Ph.D
ISBN 0-89638-190-0

A Journey Through Grief–Book
Gentle, Specific Help to Get You through the Most Difficult Stages of Grieving
by Alla Renée Bozarth, Ph.D
ISBN 0-89638-204-4

Dance For Me When I Die–Audio
Death as a Rite of Passage
by Alla Renée Bozarth, Ph.D
ISBN 0-89638-135-8

A Day at a Time
Daily Reflections for Recovering People
ISBN 0-89638-196-X

Daddy, Please Say You're Sorry
One Woman's Journey of Healing from Sexual Abuse
by Amber
ISBN 0-89638-262-1

A Gentle Path Through the Twelve Steps
The Classic Guide for All People in the Process of Recovery
by Dr. Patrick Carnes
ISBN 0-89638-290-7

Order Form

Order No.	Qty.	Title	Author	Price	Total
360-1		Wisdom and Wonderment	Alla Renée Bozarth	$9.95	
115-3		Life Is Goodbye/Life Is Hello	Alla Renée Bozarth	$12.95	
204-4		A Journey Through Grief–Book	Alla Renée Bozarth	$4.95	
190-0		A Journey Through Grief–Audio	Alla Renée Bozarth	$9.95	
135-8		Dance For Me When I Die–Audio	Alla Renée Bozarth	$9.95	
126-9		A Day at a Time–Audio		$9.95	
001-7		–Deluxe Gift		$10.95	
196-X		–Paperback		$7.95	
000-9		–Classic Rust		$8.95	
262-1		Daddy, Please Say You're Sorry	Amber	$12.95	
290-7		A Gentle Path through the Twelve Steps	Patrick Carnes	$14.95	

SHIPPING/HANDLING CHARGES

Order Amount	Shipping Charges
$0.00 - $10.00	$3.50
$10.01 - $25.00	$4.00
$25.01 - $50.00	$5.00
$50.01 - $75.00	$7.00

Subtotal

Shipping and Handling (see below)

Add your state's sales tax

TOTAL

Send check or money order payable to CompCare Publishers. No cash or C.O.D.s please. Quantity discounts available. Prices subject to change without notice.

Send book(s) to:

Name_____

Address _____

City_____State_____Zip_____

❏ Check enclosed for $_____, payable to CompCare Publishers

❏ Charge my credit card   ❏ Visa   ❏ MasterCard   ❏ Discover

Account #_____Exp. Date _____

Signature_____Daytime Phone _____

CompCare® Publishers
3850 Annapolis Lane, Suite 100 • Minneapolis, MN 55447-5443
(612) 559-4800 or toll free (800) 328-3330